D0252365

Jen Hathy

About the Author

Adam Selzer is the author of more than a dozen books, including several novels and the acclaimed *Smart Aleck's Guide to American History*. While doing research for stories to tell on the ghost tours that he's run in Chicago for nearly a decade, he developed a knack for discovering new clues to old mysteries. With his trademark smart-alecky humor, he's applied himself to wading through mountains of death certificates, poring through reels and reels of newspaper archives, and occasionally sticking his head right into crumbling old tombs. He lives with his wife in a small Chicago apartment where the cats have them outnumbered and know it.

ADAM SELZER

GHOSTS of Lincoln

Discovering His Paranormal Legacy

Llewellyn Worldwide
Woodbury, Minnesota

Ghosts of Lincoln: Discovering His Paranormal Legacy © 2015 by Adam Selzer. All rights reserved. No part of this book may be used or reproduced in any manner whatsoever, including Internet usage, without written permission from Llewellyn Publications, except in the case of brief quotations embodied in critical articles and reviews.

FIRST EDITION
First Printing, 2015

Book design by Bob Gaul
Cover image courtesy Library of Congress/LC-DIG-ppmsca-19301/
    original photo Alexander Gardner
Cover design by Lisa Novak
Editing by Ed Day
Interior photos courtesy Library of Congress except "Lincoln Piano" on page 100
    © Adam Selzer, "Mumler" on page 246 © College of Psychic Studies in
    London and "Lincoln Bedroom" on page 289 © John F. Kennedy Presidential
    Library and Museum in Boston

Llewellyn Publications is a registered trademark of Llewellyn Worldwide Ltd.

Library of Congress Cataloging-in-Publication Data
Selzer, Adam.
  Ghosts of Lincoln: discovering his paranormal legacy/Adam Selzer.—First Edition.
    pages cm
  Includes bibliographical references.
  ISBN 978-0-7387-4153-6
  1. Lincoln, Abraham, 1809-1865—Psychology. 2. Spiritualism—United States—
History—19th century. 3. Parapsychology—United States—History—19th century. 4. Ghosts—United States. I. Title.
  E457.2.S464 2015
  973.7092—dc23
                    2015007854

Llewellyn Worldwide Ltd. does not participate in, endorse, or have any authority or responsibility concerning private business transactions between our authors and the public.

All mail addressed to the author is forwarded, but the publisher cannot, unless specifically instructed by the author, give out an address or phone number.

Any Internet references contained in this work are current at publication time, but the publisher cannot guarantee that a specific location will continue to be maintained. Please refer to the publisher's website for links to authors' websites and other sources.

Llewellyn Publications
A Division of Llewellyn Worldwide Ltd.
2143 Woodvale Drive
Woodbury, MN 55125-2989
www.llewellyn.com

Printed in the United States of America

Contents

Introduction

*O*n January 30th, 1862, a strange ship was launched in Green Point Wharf. An ironclad battleship powered by steam and armed with guns mounted in a rotating turret, the *Monitor* was the Union's answer to the *Merrimack*, the fearsome Confederate ironclad that was under construction in the South. The Confederate ship hadn't been completed, but the Union knew it was coming. President Lincoln had overruled the Navy officials who believed it would never float, and wanted the ability to fight an ironclad with an ironclad. Even today, the *Monitor* looks like a bizarre craft, with only about eighteen inches of it visible above the water, not counting the gun turret. It would eventually be compared to a cheese box floating on a raft.

It was a strange time that called for strange solutions.

Few of the most famous battles of the Civil War had yet been fought. The battles of Fort Sumter and Bull Run (aka Manassas) had shown people that this war between Northern and Southern states was not going to be a mere thirty-day dust-up, but the bloodiest battles—those that would end with tens of thousands of casualties—were still to come. In many ways, the launching of the *Monitor* marked the war's passage from an old-fashioned war to a modern one. As soon is it took to the water, every wooden navy in the world was obsolete. The arms race that followed as nations began to update their military would boil over into the First World War half a century later.

Meanwhile, that same month, January of 1862, actor John Wilkes Booth was lodging at the Tremont House hotel in Chicago. Abraham Lincoln stayed there when he was in town, too; he had given a version of his "House Divided" speech from the balcony in 1858 and held a public reception in the lobby after his election in 1860. Now Booth was making his home there while playing a highly successful run of shows at the nearby McVicker's Theatre. During that cold winter, he starred in a different play nightly, appearing as characters such as Richard III (who kills his way to the throne), and Hamlet (who spends the whole play plotting to kill the king).

On the day the *Monitor* was launched, Booth took a break from Shakespeare and played Duke Pescara in *The Apostate*, an 1817 melodrama by Richard Sheil that was already nearly forgotten in 1862. The Duke was one of Booth's father's old roles, and is a consummate melodrama villain who seems as though he ought to be curling his mustache every time he talks. Consider the scene in which he bids Florinda to agree to marry him so he'll stop torturing her lover:

> I'll hunt for life in every trembling limb,
> and chase it down. The driving steel shall plunge—
> Nay, do not stop your ears, for his shrill screams
> shall pierce the solid deafness of the tomb.
> … Look there, look there! He dies! See where he dies!
> The wheel goes round—see, the red froth of blood!
> His hair stands up, and drips with agony![1]

The play isn't as bad as it's sometimes made out to be today (it's pretty entertaining once it gets going, especially if you read Pescara's lines in a Darth Vader voice), but it's seldom read anymore, probably hasn't been performed in years, and is really only remembered because of Booth's connection to it. He played the same role in Albany, New York, the night Lincoln came through en route to Washington a year before, and he would play it again in 1865 in his last performance at Ford's Theatre in Washington.

The night after he appeared in *The Apostate*, Booth played a regicidal role that has aged better, and which the *Chicago Tribune* said was his personal favorite: *Macbeth*.[2]

Besides just the choice in Chicago hotels, Lincoln and Booth had another thing in common: *Macbeth* was Lincoln's favorite, too.

Though much of what we say and write and think about Abraham Lincoln today is based on guesswork and bad sources, we know that our sixteenth president was a *Macbeth* man beyond all doubt. In an 1863 letter to actor James Hackett,[3] Lincoln wrote that "Some of Shakespeare's plays I have never read; while others I have gone over perhaps as frequently as any unprofessional reader. Among the latter are *Lear, Richard III, Henry VIII, Hamlet,* and especially *Macbeth.* I think nothing equals *Macbeth.* It is wonderful."

Macbeth certainly kept a hold on Lincoln's mind throughout his presidency. On April 9, 1865—five days before Booth would assassinate him at Ford's Theatre—Lincoln was sailing back to Washington aboard the *River Queen* after a triumphant visit to Richmond, the recently vacated Confederate capital, and passed the time by reading out loud from a handsome quarto of Shakespeare plays.

Lincoln in February 1865. Courtesy Library of Congress.

Memoirs of the journey were later recorded by the Marquis de Chambrun and Sen. Charles Sumner, members of the traveling party. It's difficult to read either of their accounts without getting the impression that Lincoln must have known on some subconscious level that his life was coming to an end. Even though the war was clearly coming to an end, he was overcome by melancholy and depression (perhaps owing to the fact that he'd spent much of the day visiting hospitals full of maimed soldiers), and death was certainly on his mind as he sailed along.

"Most of the (passages)," Chambrun wrote, "were from *Macbeth*, and, in particular, the verses which follow Duncan's assassination ... either because he was struck by the weird beauty of these verses, or from a vague presentiment coming over him."[4]

Only days after the trip, Senator Sumner would tell the same story of Lincoln reading from *Macbeth* in his eulogy for the slain president, and he pointed out the exact passage that seemed to inspire some "vague presentiment" in the president's mind:

> Duncan is in his grave;
> after life's fitful fever, he sleeps well
> Treason has done his worst; nor steel, not poison,
> Malice domestic, foreign levy,
> nothing can touch him further.

"Impressed by their beauty or by some presentiment unuttered," Sumner continued, "he read them aloud a second time. As the friends who then surrounded him listened to his reading, they little thought how, in a few days, what was said of the murdered Duncan would be said of him. Nothing can touch him further."[5]

And here's one more strange fact about the play that touched Lincoln so, and was a favorite role of Booth, Lincoln's eventual killer: according to the *Oxford English Dictionary*, Act 1, Scene 7 of *Macbeth*, contains the earliest known use of the word "assassination."

So, what does it all mean?

Nothing, really. After all, the fact that *Macbeth* is the earliest printed use of the word doesn't necessarily mean that Shakespeare invented it. Like a lot of "coined by Shakespeare" words and phrases, this is simply the earliest documented use.

Looked at from a certain angle, though, it's easy to see psychic connections and eerie coincidences in the odd attachments Lincoln and Booth both had to *Macbeth*. Those given to thinking such things can surely imagine that it's evidence of a grand design or that Lincoln's attraction to the play, and to those lines in particular less than a week before his death, speak to a sort of latent psychic hunch about the nature of his own demise. Or perhaps even that Booth had picked up on some sort of mental energy Lincoln left behind in the Tremont House lobby.

Lincoln lore is like this in general. If you research stories of our sixteenth president and the Civil War long enough, everything seems supernatural. There's a reason some historians quite seriously refer to Lincoln as a prophet, not a mere mortal.

And whether one believes in the paranormal or not, Lincoln has had a profound impact on the way we, as a society, think of ghosts, psychics, and communication with the dead. Perhaps only Shakespeare himself influenced our concept of the supernatural more. It may have been through no fault of Lincoln's own (certainly his views on religious and supernatural matters are up for debate), but stories of Lincoln haunting the White House and predicting his own assassination, along with the many mysteries surrounding his life and legacy, are a part of our national folklore. By now, Lincoln almost seems like a supernatural visitor to our nation. He came from nowhere, achieved the impossible, and then was gone.

Researching him today is very much like chasing a ghost—he appears everywhere, but is impossible to quite pin down. If you follow the footnotes in the endless stream of Lincoln books, you find that even many of the most respected biographies of him make use of a lot of sources that can hardly be counted as reliable. We don't really know what made the man tick, what his motivations were, or what all of his views might be in the twenty-first century—and we've never tired of trying to figure it out. He's as mysterious as any ghost story.

It's difficult now to determine just when Lincoln started to seem like a human being and took on the sheen of a legend; many say it started the moment he was shot, but articles about him written in the weeks beforehand, when Congress had approved the Thirteenth Amendment outlawing slavery and General Lee had surrendered, make it seem like it was already going on by then. Scroll through some accounts of what went on at the Republican Convention of 1860, the year he was first nominated, and you'll come away thinking that he was more legend than man even before he was president.

A century and a half later, Lincoln has been portrayed as both a deeply religious man and as a profound doubter who was not really a Christian at all; as the biggest racist on the planet, and as the best friend the black race ever had; as a hardcore abolitionist, and a man who was soft on slavery or even a slave-owner himself (a common myth that just won't die). He's been looked upon as both a liberal and a conservative, a socialist and a fascist, a warmonger and a wimp. Since he died before he could write memoirs and comment on his motivations and goals himself, historians have been left to fill in the blanks. Biographers were collecting anecdotes for books before his body was cold.

And when personal recollections of Lincoln ran out, his friends having died off or told all they remembered, stories of his ghost began to circulate.

It's almost a running joke that Lincoln seems to be haunting a lot of places, as though he was the Johnny Appleseed of ghosts, leaving spirits in his wake wherever he traveled (and a few places where he didn't). Lincoln scholar Harold Holzer once said "I've heard Lincoln haunts the rail lines...I've also heard he haunts the Lincoln room at the White House and his old house in Springfield. Now, either Lincoln is the most peripatetic ghost in the country or people think every tall ghost is Lincoln."[6]

But if we make the broad hypothetical leap and assume that ghosts and spirits are real in the first place, who says a person can only have one ghost? The idea that the things we call ghosts are someone's immortal spirit or soul is only one of the endless theories about where the things we call ghosts come from. That a person could leave behind traces of himself that people might be able to pick up all over the place squares with several pseudoscientific theories that seek to explain the paranormal. And even if the "ghosts" people see of Lincoln are all in their head, the product of their brains processing the impact Lincoln continues to have on us, why shouldn't that count as a ghost? Ghost hunting isn't like Bigfoot hunting. Bigfoot either exists or he doesn't, and that's all there is to it. With ghosts, there's more of a gray area. What counts as a ghost?

It's fair to say that Lincoln haunts the United States, whether as an actual ghost, as several different ghosts, or as just a strange, unknowable presence in our collective mind and memory. His life and work changed nearly every aspect of the nation, and his death changed more of them still (his elaborate, cross-country funeral almost single-handedly created the modern funeral industry).

Mysteries about him continue to fascinate us: Was Ann Rutledge really his true love? Did he love Mary, his wife, at all? Was he a religious man? What did his voice really sound like?

Is the stovepipe hat on display at the museum in Springfield really his? Did he use the term "under God" in the Gettysburg address? (It appears in some transcripts, but not in others.)

And then there are the paranormal questions: Is his ghost really haunting the White House? Did he predict his own death? Did others predict it for him? Did he get advice about freeing the slaves from mediums channeling the spirits of our founding fathers? Did his own spirit come back and speak to us through mediums later?

It's never my intention to prove or debunk a ghost story; instead, with this book, as with most of my research into ghost lore, I simply intend to examine the backstory. I wish to determine what we really know and what we don't about Lincoln's connection to the supernatural (both before and after his death), and about the stories about his ghost appearing all over the country, in and out of seances.

I've probably just thrown cold water on a few stories about Lincoln, including one or two that have become a part of our cultural imagination.

But I think I've found a couple of new ones as well, and new evidence about old stories that may strengthen their credibility.

Researching this book has been equal parts frustrating and fascinating—Lincoln research always is. For every source, there's an equal but opposite source, and scarcely any anecdote about him really holds up to intense scrutiny. Following the footnotes of a Lincoln book can drive you toward madness. But it also gives you the chance to spend days trying to determine whether Lincoln might have actually taken a ride on a flying piano, and that's a damned interesting way to spend one's working life.

One

A World of Superstition

Long about 1815, a group of women in LaRue County, Kentucky, stood around a slanting rock to gossip while they did their laundry. On this particular day, the conversation turned to the subject of dreams.

"Don't tell your dreams before breakfast," said one young woman. "You know I dreamed Aunt Mary Kastor was dead, told it before breakfast, and within a week we buried her. I wouldn't tell another bad dream before breakfast for anything."

Another woman nearby related a story of dreaming about a man drowning in the nearby Rolling Fork River, and of waking her husband up in the middle of the night (well before breakfast) to tell him about it. "And just three weeks after that," she said, "they found a man's body, all covered with mud, on the banks of the river."

Another woman told of a dream she'd had in which gold had been discovered in the nearby hills, and in which President James Madison had come from "Washington City" to oversee the workers digging gold out of the hills so that he could use it to pay for roads that were to be built from one end of the country to the other.

One boy of about six listened intently, and asked the woman, Mrs. Gollaher, if she "believed there was anything in dreams."

"Yes," Mrs. Gollaher replied, "but you and Austin mustn't look for gold in that hill, because you might get lost."

"I don't want any gold," the young boy replied. "The reason I asked you if you believe dreams come true was because I once had a dream which I have been thinking about a heap."

"Was it about your sweetheart?" a woman asked.

"No, ma'am," said the boy. "I haven't got any sweetheart. I did have one, but she said my feet and hands were too big, and my legs and arms too long, and that she liked the Evans boy better than she did me, so Susie—Susie Enlow—don't like me anymore."

"That's too bad," said a woman. "But we want to hear about your dream. What was it?"

"Well," he said, "my dream was about making a speech to a lot of people in a big town, and … there wasn't much more to it."

"Do you ever expect to make a speech to a lot of people in a big town?" asked Mrs. Gollaher.

"I don't know," said the boy. "I might."[7]

The young boy, as you've surely guessed, was Abraham Lincoln, perhaps giving an early example of the prophetic gifts he would one day be said to have. By 1858, he was giving speeches to as many as twenty thousand people at a time in towns big and small.

The story is a good one to look at simply as an example of just how hard it is to find reliable information about anything to do with Abraham Lincoln. The source on the tale of young Abe dreaming of making a speech in a big town is a reasonably solid one—it came straight from the mouth of Austin Gollaher, who is mentioned by his mother in the story and was Abraham Lincoln's neighbor and boyhood friend. It is, it would appear, a first-hand, eyewitness account.

However, it survives only in a book by J. Rogers Gore, a *LaRue County Herald* reporter, entitled *The Boyhood of Abraham Lincoln: From the Spoken Narratives of Austin Gollaher*. It wasn't published until 1921, more than two decades after Gollaher's death in 1898, and well over a century after James Madison's presidency. The stories in it are generally not taken seriously by historians, and tend not to hold up very well to fact-checking. For instance, records show that there was an Enlow family in the area (it was widely rumored at one time that Mr. Enlow was Abraham's true biological father) but not that they had a daughter named Susie. In fact, it's hard to picture young Abe being able to imagine what a big town looked like at the age of six. Had he ever even seen any of the world outside of the hills and forests of Kentucky in those days? Could he picture what the world was like outside of LaRue County at all?

Austin Gollaher, though, was a real person who definitely knew young Abe Lincoln; late in his life, he told several first-hand accounts of what Lincoln was like as a boy. His stories are generally not regarded as entirely trustworthy, though—he doesn't seem to have told anyone his stories until decades after the fact, and after journalists discovered him his stories got more elaborate as the years went by. The details of young Lincoln's conversation about dreams are almost certainly embellishments by a reporter on Gore's part, though it may be that Gollaher at least told him that he remembered Lincoln dreaming of making speeches as a five-year-old, and the story does give us some sense of the superstitious world Lincoln lived in as a young man.

A somewhat more reliable story about Austin and Abe's friendship—my favorite story in all of Lincoln lore—is actually a second- or third-hand source collected by William Herndon, Lincoln's law partner in Springfield who became his first biographer. According to Chas Friend, another LaRue County native who used to send Herndon anecdotes he collected around town, a doctor from LaRue named Jesse Reardon visited Lincoln in the White House to discuss matters related to the draft, and President Lincoln asked about all of the old families he remembered. After asking about the Cessnas, the Brownfields, and the Fitzpatricks, the president came to the subject of the Gollahers, and related a charming, earthy sort of story:

"Where is my old friend and playmate Austin Gollaher?" he asked. "I would rather see Gollaher than any man living; he played me a dirty trick once and I want to pay him up. One Sunday, Gollaher and another boy and myself were out in the woods on Knob Creek playing and hunting around for young squirrels when I climbed up a tree and left Austin and the other boy on the ground. Gollaher shut his eyes like he was asleep. I noticed his hat sat straight with the reverse side up, (and) I thought I would shit in his hat. Gollaher was watching, and when I let the load drop he swapped hats and my hat caught the whole charge!"

"At this recital," Friend wrote, "The President laughed heartily."[8]

Chas Friend himself is not thought of as the most reliable of Herndon's sources (and Herndon himself seems to have been a bit remiss when it came to fact-checking, especially when a story emphasized the slavery-hating "diamond glowing in the dunghill" angle he wanted to emphasize when talking about Lincoln's formative years). Friend was thirty-two years younger than Abraham Lincoln, and wasn't born until years after the Lincolns had left the area. He merely acted as gatherer of anecdotes that he'd collect from older locals, and which he'd then mail to Herndon in letters marked by spelling that was so wild as to qualify as a sort of outsider art. Much of the material was strictly gossipy;

earlier in the same letter as the hat story, he was occupied with various rumors that Lincoln was not truly the son of Thomas Lincoln, including some particularly juicy gossip about Thomas Lincoln's "testacles."

Still, the Gollaher story he sent to Herndon predates the time when Gollaher was discovered by journalists, and is the kind of story that it's hard to imagine Friend simply making up. The story is exactly the sort of yarn that Lincoln liked to tell, though early biographers made a conscious effort to cover up the fact that he loved dirty jokes.

And here, in a nutshell, we have the problem of researching the life of Abraham Lincoln: even first- and second-hand accounts of his character tend to be unreliable, and sometimes sources that seem bad might be better than they look. A first-hand eyewitness account of Lincoln telling the story of a strange dream can sometimes be less reliable than a third-hand story about him pooping in hats.

But whatever drawbacks they may have about giving us actual details about Lincoln's boyhood, Herndon's many sources of anecdotes do give us a vivid portrait of what sort of world Lincoln was raised in, a world that's very difficult for us to imagine today. His biological mother, Nancy Hanks, came from a type of family that Herndon said was common to early Kentucky; "Illiterate and superstitious," he wrote, "they corresponded to that nomadic class still to be met throughout the South and known as 'poor whites.'"[9]

Theirs was a world where shoes were only worn when it was absolutely necessary and when families, though scattered wide apart, would often make great journeys in order to gather together simply to dance and drink whiskey, which seems to have been among the more common pastimes. Dennis Hanks, a cousin of Lincoln's mother, is described as wandering home from rural parties expressing typical early American rough-and-tumble patriotism by singing out a song of his own composition: "Hail Columbia, happy land! If you ain't drunk, then I'll be damned!"[10]

Theirs was an isolated, rural life in a world of death, disease, roughhousing, and booze, far removed from society at large. Superstition, wrote Herndon, was rural Kentucky's food and drink.

"They believed," he wrote, "in the baneful influence of witches, pinned their faith to the curative power of wizards in dealing with sick animals, and shot the image of a witch with a silver ball to break the spell she was supposed to have over human beings. They followed with religious minuteness the directions of the water-wizard, with his magic divining rod, and the faith doctor who wrought miraculous cures by strange sounds and signals to some mysterious agency. The flight of a bird in at the window, the breath of a horse on a child's head, the crossing by a dog of a hunter's path, all betokened evil luck in store for some one. The moon exercised greater influence on the actions of the people and the growth of vegetation than the sun and all the planetary system combined. Fence rails could only be cut in the light of the moon, and potatoes could be planted only in the dark of the moon. Trees and plants which bore their fruit above ground could be planted when the moon shone full. Soap could only be made in the light of the moon, and it must only be stirred in one way and by one person. They had the horror of Friday which with many exists to this day. Nothing was to be begun on that unlucky day, for if the rule were violated an endless train of disasters was sure to follow. Surrounded by people who believed in these things, Lincoln grew to manhood. With them he walked, talked, and labored, and from them he also absorbed whatever of superstition showed itself in him thereafter." [11]

Of course, Herndon doesn't seem to elaborate on just where he heard these particular superstitions, and further doesn't seem to give a source on his later claim that "listening in boyish wonder to the legends of some toothless old dame led him to believe the significance of dreams and visions," so we can't necessarily be sure that Herndon wasn't just making Kentucky look awful so Lincoln's adulthood would look all the more amazing to his readers. Then again, perhaps this was an allusion to one of the women who lived near the Lincolns, perhaps even one of the same women who appear in the anecdote about Lincoln listening to women talking about dreams while they did laundry (missing teeth would have surely been the norm among the older neighbors). Perhaps Lincoln even chatted with Herndon about it during late nights at the office.

In any case, it's probably not far off from reality, and it was in this backwoods environment that Lincoln grew up, and it surely shaped his way of looking at the world, whether he truly believed in any of the superstitions himself.

J. Rogers Gore records a couple of stories about ghosts and legends in his book *The Boyhood of Abraham Lincoln*, that were allegedly collected from Gollaher (though Gore no doubt embellished them a bit).

One of his stories tells of "ghost of the woods" which was not the ghost of a person, but a tree—a huge white trunk of a dead tree that stood atop Muldraugh Hill, five miles from Lincoln's home. Stripped of all bark "by Old Father Time," with two remaining limbs and a massive knot that looked like a human head, some people believed that the tree had a consciousness of its own, and that the position and shape of its branches in the wind could be interpreted as warnings or omens. "The more simple minded," Gollaher reported (through Gore), "would climb the hill to commune with the old white trunk whose spirit had passed on, and…bring home with them tales which opened wide the children's eyes and sent them creeping fearfully to bed." A man Gollaher referred to as Old Man Pottinger claimed to have seen the tree smoking a pipe, which he saw as a sign that the end of the world was near. "They had to tie him to his bed and keep him there til he died," Gollaher noted.

One day, Austin suggested to Abe that they go climb the hill and see if the tree was still there. Young Abe professed that he didn't believe in it even as Austin claimed that the branches were probably pointing to that hill full of gold from his mother's dream, and that they could get rich. But Abe was obstinate. "If I wanted to believe in a tree," he said, "I'd choose a big live one with leaves on it."

Only days after this conversation, according to Gollaher (via Rogers), the body of a mutilated man was found at the foot of the hill Austin had tried to get Abe to visit. He had been shot through the head, possibly by his own gun, and torn apart by wild animals.[12]

The volume Gore compiled also contained a bit of talk of more standard ghosts—a new neighbor who was given to pranks moved to town and once came to the Lincoln homestead dressed as a "ghost" with a long, white robe and an ox head that she used as a mask. In Gore's retelling, Thomas Lincoln was terrified, but young Abe, who had seen the ox head at the new neighbors' house the day before, casually walked behind her and lifted the ox head off, revealing the new neighbor (who would have gotten away with it if it weren't for that meddling kid). The next day, Abe told Austin that "Father doesn't exactly believed in ghosts, but he says he has seen funny things in the woods at night, and for that reason he doesn't like to be out after dark. Once he was sure he saw an Indian war-dance . . . (once) he told mother he saw a giant riding a big lion through the woods. Mother put father to bed, and he didn't get out for a long time."[13]

Even here, Lincoln is portrayed as skeptical and level-headed, but that Lincoln took stock in the significance of dreams, visions, and omens from time to time throughout his life is actually well established. Little things—some of them remarkably well sourced—show that he did hang on to something of a belief in folk remedies which, even at the time, must have seemed more like magic and superstition than actual medicine. In particular, a couple of early sources write that Lincoln was willing to put some stock in the belief in "mad stones," a common cure for rabies of the day. More properly known as bezoars, "mad stones" are rocklike, concentrated hairballs taken from the stomachs of animals—usually deer or dogs—that look … well (if I may put aside any scholarly pretensions for a moment), they look like Easter eggs made out of turds. They've long been applied to dog bites in attempt to cure rabies—the "stone" would be boiled in milk until the milk turned green, then applied directly to the wound.

Judge Joseph Gillespie, a friend of Lincoln throughout his adult life, wrote to Herndon that Lincoln "had great faith in the strong sense of Country People and he gave them credit for greater intelligence than most men do. If he found an idea prevailing generally amongst them he believed there was something in it, although it might not harmonize with science. He had great faith in the virtues of the mad stone, although he could give no reason for it, and confessed that it looked like superstition. But he said he found the people in the neighborhood of these stones fully impressed with a belief in their virtues from actual experiment."[14]

Lincoln may have even attempted to try out a mad stone himself. Frances Wallace, one of his sisters-in-law, told Herndon that when Lincoln's son, Robert, was bitten by a rabid dog, Abe took him clear to Terre Haute, Indiana, for treatment with a mad stone. Details are scarce, but this trip is sometimes said to have happened as late as 1859, when Lincoln was on the cusp of the presidency.

Whether the use of the mad stone would really be superstition, not "medicine" by nineteenth-century standards, is probably up for debate. Rabies was not easily treatable at the time, and the mad stone probably seemed like as good a remedy as any; certainly the application of it couldn't hurt anything. In a 1936 article in the *Indiana Magazine of History*, Max Ehrmann suggested that the stone cured bites not due to magic, but "because it was a porous stone. When placed on a wound it would by capillary attraction draw out moisture, blood, and probably the poison."[15]

In any case, it does seem likely that some of the superstitions he grew up around in his Kentucky boyhood left Lincoln with an open mind about such matters later in life.

Lincoln as a Young Man

The exact reasons for Thomas Lincoln's move from Kentucky to Indiana when Lincoln was young vary from source to source, ranging from Thomas losing his land due to bad property titles (which was certainly a factor) to a desire to move from a slave state to a free state (Lincoln himself would claim that this was a factor when he wrote a short autobiography for publicity purposes after his surprise nomination for the presidency in 1860). Abraham's mother died two years after the move, and Thomas remarried, this time to Sarah Bush Johnston, whom Lincoln would always call "mother."

Stories of his boyhood in Indiana contain many familiar yarns about him working as a rail splitter, doing chores, and reading anything he could get his hands on. It was Sarah, in her twilight years, who first told the famous story of him doing "sums" on the back of a coal shovel by the firelight in attempt to educate himself. Exactly how much formal education Abraham had is a matter of some dispute, but it certainly wasn't much. Still, in his own words, he somehow learned to "read, write, and cipher to the rule of three,"[16] and even behaved like a regular schoolboy in his own "sums book," writing down a bit of a joke in the margins:

Abraham Lincoln is my name
And with my pen I wrote the same
I wrote it in both haste and speed
And left it here for fools to read.[17]

Little could he have dreamed that he'd still be trolling "fools" who looked up pictures of the sum book nearly two centuries later.

The family remained in Indiana until 1830, when an outbreak of "milk sick" led them to move west into Illinois, the state that would be Abraham's home for the next thirty years. By this time, he was a young man, and it may have been around this time that he was first prophesied to become president some day.

In 1831, he took a job hauling goods down the river to New Orleans, and while in that city, it is said, he visited a "voodoo negress" with his companion, John Hanks. According to legend, the voodoo doctor "became much excited" upon examining Lincoln, and told him, "You will be president, and all the negroes will be free."[18]

Of course, this story didn't begin to circulate until well after both parts of the prophecy had already come true, but it seems to have been circulating by word of mouth for some time before it was published. When Herndon's collaborator asked Hanks about it, Hanks said that he and Lincoln had been in New Orleans together several times, but that "I Dont Now (sic) whether he got his fortune told or not."[19] That Lincoln visited a fortune-teller in New Orleans, at least as a lark, is entirely possible, but if his fortune was that he'd become president ... well, it's not hard to imagine that the fortune-teller probably told that to all the ambitious young men who paid their fee. Isaac Newton Arnold wrote the story in his book *The Life of Abraham Lincoln* in 1885, but included a footnote speaking of correspondence with Herndon in which both expressed doubt about it. Both, though, were also willing to entertain the notion that this "prophecy" had first planted the seed in Lincoln's mind that grew into his later ambitions.

Back in Illinois after the New Orleans trip, young Lincoln had his famous courtship with Ann Rutledge, whom he may have wished to marry, though such plans were dashed when she died of typhoid fever in 1835. He met Mary Ann Todd in 1839, became engaged to her in 1840, and married her, following a sort of rocky courtship, in 1842. The two had been set to marry the year before, but the wedding had been called off, and exactly why they decided to marry later is not entirely known; while preparing for the wedding, Lincoln was supposedly asked where he was going, and replied "To hell, I suppose."[20]

Whether their marriage was a happy one depends a lot on which source you're reading, though very few early biographers had anything nice to say about Mary. It's common now to hear that her poor treatment by early writers is just a result of Victorian misogyny, which surely played a part, but it's also hard to study her at all without getting the idea that she was a very difficult woman to live with. We do know that when Lincoln became a lawyer, he spent twenty weeks a year traveling "the circuit," practicing in rural towns, and that this kept him away from Mary for long stretches of time. Some believe that that was the whole point of working the job, which he kept up long after he could afford to stay home.

In any case, he prospered as a lawyer in Springfield, had four children with Mary, served briefly in the military during the Black Hawk War (where, as a captain, he had his first real chance to display his skills as a leader) and served a term in the United States Congress as a member of the Whig party during the Mexican-American War (which he opposed). While there, he served with former president John Quincy Adams, who had returned to the House of Representatives.

To say John Quincy Adams himself had a remarkable career is to understate matters. The son of Founding Father and former president John Adams, Quincy was appointed the United States Minister to the Netherlands by George Washington at the age of twenty-six. He had been Secretary of State, a senator, and the sixth president. After his presidency, he took a seat in the House of Representatives, where he spent the rest of his life attacking slavery.

He is probably the only man who worked with both Lincoln and the Founding Fathers, but he couldn't have possibly guessed that anyone would ever say that about him. Lincoln's single two-year term was generally undistinguished, and no record survives of what former President Adams thought of him, if he took any real notice of him at all. Stories that he took Lincoln under his wing and mentored him, perhaps bringing him into the anti-slavery cause, are entirely fanciful; Adams was an old man, barely strong enough to speak, in the few months he and Lincoln served in the same Congress before his death.

After his single term, Abraham Lincoln declined to seek re-election, knowing his opposition to the Mexican-American

War had probably spoiled his chances, and returned to his law practice in Springfield. Eventually, people began to speak of him as a candidate for the United States Senate, and he came very close to being named the senator by the state legislature (which was how people became senators in Illinois at the time; popular election of them is a relatively recent notion).

Looking back on Abraham Lincoln's early biography, it really is remarkable to consider that this was a man who would be elected president one day. The United States was a new country when Lincoln was born, and it would still be a generation or two before a president who was not firmly aristocratic to begin with would be elected. Even as late as the 1850s, when the country seemed ready to split apart, it would have seemed nearly impossible that such an obscure figure could become president, and it's unlikely that Lincoln seriously considered the possibility of being nominated for the job, though he was certainly ambitious and knew he had an outside chance.

But perhaps people really had been telling him that one day he would be president. The "voodoo" story is only one of several stories about premonitions regarding Lincoln's destiny that have circulated over the years.

He was a man destined to change the world, and, at least after the fact, plenty of people claimed to have known it all along.

Two

Early Premonitions

During the summer of 1860, while Lincoln's representatives promoted his candidacy for president, people all over the northern states witnessed the Great Meteor of 1860, a very rare "Earth grazing" procession of meteors that looked like a fireball blazing across the evening sky. The phenomenon was described by one witness as "The grandest meteor we ever had the fortune to see ... (it) made its way through the heavens to the wonderment of every mortal with eyesight who was out of doors at the time ... we were standing, at the moment, in the shadow of buildings that completely shut out the western sky. A flood of light, like that of a vivid, continuous flash of lightning, or like a bright dawn, streamed over the tops of the houses, and grew in intensity for a few seconds, ere the majestic orb sailed sublimely into sight overhead. Over the zenith it sped, reddish in hue, and with a wake of fire that spanned the sky for an instant like a vast arch of celestial flame."[21]

According to a 1931 history of Hamilton County, Tennesee,[22] a crowd in Chattanooga, Tennessee, gathered in an open grove to see a speaker and instead saw the meteor pass by. It was said that the meteor appeared to split into two parts as it flew over the Tennessee sky, and some present declared that it was an omen that the country would soon be split into two parts as well.

Most accounts of the 1860 fireball say it was only really visible in the North, though I did find an August 1860 letter in a South Carolina newspaper describing seeing a brilliant, Roman candle-like meteor from Lookout Mountain, overlooking Chattanooga.[23] No mention was made of it being an omen there, but plenty of papers did see the meteor as a harbinger of ill times ahead.

In the typical fiery rhetoric of its Lincoln-hating editor, Wilbur F. Storey, the *Chicago Times* saw it as a particularly grim sign: "Recorded history does not present a warning so wonderful and palpable!" Storey wrote. "Who can fail to perceive in the variegated lights of the meteor rising in the Northwest, the typification of the conglomerated isms headed by Lincoln? Who can fail to comprehend the lesson recorded by all the past history of omens, that these fiery messengers portend the approach of war, revolution, and change? Who fails to recognise the almost equal division of the meteor in mid-heaven, over the American Union, the disseverance of the Confederacy? If heaven has at all spoken to this self-doomed land, its warning has been written on the sky in the language that a child might understand."[24]

As a before-the-fact prediction, it's really pretty impressive—it actually even uses the words "union" and "confederacy" in the same sentence, months before that was the official name of the Confederate States of America.

Less successful as soothsayers were the *Boston Herald*, who said "(The Meteor) came from the Northwest (like Lincoln and Douglas), but whether it is an omen for the success of Douglas or the defeat of Lincoln we cannot say . . . it went out as quick as 'Old Abe's' star will next November."[25]

Of course, by July of 1860, predicting that the country would soon split into two was about like predicting that a football team that was ahead by forty-two points at the end of the third quarter was going to win the game. It required no particular psychic powers. By then, with Lincoln cruising toward the presidency (no matter what the *Herald* said) and southern states threatening to secede if he won, the split seemed almost inevitable.

Some assigned more specific omens to the meteor. A Sacramento paper speculated that this was a new visitation of the same comet that had been seen by Emperor Charles V three centuries before that had been deemed a sign of his impending death, just as the same comet had been a sign of the death of Pope Urban IV three centuries before that.[26]

The meteor, in any case, was only one of the stories of omens and dreams that were said (usually after some time had passed) to be celestial warnings of a dark future for both the nation and its new president, Abraham Lincoln.

Of course, not everyone spoke of omens quite so seriously. Take, for instance, Sen. Stephen Douglas himself, Lincoln's debate rival in 1858 and rival candidate for president in 1860. Once, in a speech defending the Fugitive Slave Act, which required captured runaway slaves in non-slave states to be returned to their owners (a highly controversial law that forced northerners who'd previously been able to ignore slavery to confront it), Douglas actually used the superstitions of Africans as a reason why slavery was well within "God's laws," stating that "The history of the world furnishes few examples where any considerable portion of the human race have shown themselves significantly enlightened and civilized to exercise the rights and enjoy the blessings of freedom. In Asia and Africa we find nothing but ignorance, superstition, and despotism." [27]

One imagines, though, that Douglas didn't have the same scorn for the *Chicago Times* and their superstitions about the Meteor of 1860. The paper basically existed to promote him in those days.

Senator Douglas has a complicated legacy as a politician, to say the very least. He brought the railroads to Chicago, essentially making the mud-hole village on the prairie into the city that would one day nominate Lincoln for president (an event that probably couldn't have happened in any other city, as we shall see). And when he ran against Lincoln for president in 1860, he effectively dropped out of the campaign halfway through, realizing that Lincoln was going to win, and traveled through the South on a mission to keep the southern states from seceding from the Union, as they were by then threatening to do. It was a noble move, truly putting the needs of the country ahead of his own ambitions. Even Lincoln, his greatest rival, held him in high esteem privately—the two were sort of friendly enemies, debating publicly and ruthlessly in campaigns against one another, though they also traveled and dined together, and visited one another's homes.

But Douglas's views on race and slavery are a giant smear on his reputation. Nobody in the nineteenth century can honestly be expected to have views on race that hold up to today's standards, but even by nineteenth-century standards, Douglas has a pretty bad record.

Though some tend to downplay the role slavery held in sparking the Civil War, it's pretty much impossible to read vintage books, newspaper articles, and letters that touch on the rift between northern and southern states and think that the conflict had any other root at all. Look at the songs people sang, the letters they wrote, the articles they read, or the speeches they heard and you'll get the distinct impression that everyone knew that the war was about slavery, even

long before the abolition of the institution became a formal, or plausible, goal on the Union's part. Reports about
the Meteor of 1860 in southern papers tend to be buried
among endless condemnations of Lincoln and the abolitionists, defenses of slavery, and instances of the northern
states resisting the fugitive slave law, all held up as proof
that secession would be a necessary step to preserving the
institution. It was practically all some papers talked about
that year.

Indeed, the conflict between slave states and free states
had been raging ever since the states were still colonies—
arguments about the institution had nearly derailed the
drafting of the Declaration of Independence in 1776. Lincoln
maintained that the Founding Fathers sought to contain slavery on the assumption that it would die out on its own as
long as they didn't let it spread (though, then as now, claiming
that the Founding Fathers agreed on anything was somewhat
disingenuous). By the 1850s, it was often said that no debate
about anything could go more than a few minutes without
turning into a debate on slavery.

And it was Douglas, in fact, who truly lit the powder
keg that blew the issue from a topic that inspired heated
debate to a topic that inspired violence.

Since the early days of the nation, slave states had been
eager to add more slave states to the Union, and non-slave
states had been equally eager to add more free states; both

sides wanted to have more votes than the other in Congress. As the country added more and more states and the debate grew tiresome, forces in Congress agreed to the Missouri Compromise in 1820, which determined that henceforth, states south of Missouri would be slave states, and states north of it would not be. This didn't end the debate about slavery, but it quieted it down somewhat, since there wasn't a new battle over it every time a new state was admitted. But it turned the debate firmly into a North-South issue, officially making the country, as Lincoln would later put it, "half slave and half free."

It was Stephen Douglas who designed the Kansas-Nebraska Act, which repealed the Missouri Compromise and made it so that white male voters in new territories would determine for themselves whether slavery would be allowed within their borders. It would be fair to say that the act was controversial; when he spoke about the law in Chicago, he was pelted with raw produce. The *Tribune* later said that "in the melee that followed, nearly everybody got another man's hat."[28, 29]

Stephen Douglas was known as the "Little Giant."
There are brochures about him set up on top of the sarcophagus
in his tomb today. Courtesy Library of Congress.

When Kansas was admitted to the Union, pro-slavery militias known as "border ruffians" actually traveled there, determined to make Kansas a slave state by any means necessary. The "Bloody Kansas" battles that followed would later seem like warm-ups for the Civil War (one such border ruffian, Martin Quinlan, later ended up working as the city cemetery manager in Chicago and was arrested for taking bribes from grave robbers in 1857—he even helped them load the plundered corpses onto their wagons to take back to the medical schools).[30]

It was in this atmosphere, with slavery debates getting progressively more violent, that Abraham Lincoln first rose to national prominence via his highly publicized 1858 debates with Douglas. As of 1854, Lincoln was back at his law practice, his political ambitions seemingly a thing of the past, but Douglas's action led him to change. "I was losing interest in politics," Lincoln wrote in 1859, "when the repeal of the Missouri Compromise aroused me again. What I have done since then is pretty well known."[31]

Some scholars believe his desire to bring about slavery's eventual end was genuine and heartfelt. Some say he merely opposed slavery for economic reasons. Others say he just read the political tea leaves and acted based on ruthless opportunism. But just as he said, what he did after 1854 is pretty well known. The fight against the spread of slavery would define the rest of his life.

*St. George's Episcopal Church, whose Civil War ghost stories
precede the war itself, as it appeared in 1864 when it was
serving as a hospital for soldiers. It's a common hub for
local ghostlore today. Courtesy Library of Congress.*

Lincoln, Douglas, and
Lincoln's Rise to the Presidency

There were some ghost stories coming up in the world as the
country slipped toward war; the first Civil War ghosts are said
to have appeared before the states even began to secede. One
story about St. George's Episcopal Church in Fredericksburg
goes clear to 1858: according to legend, a singer in the choir

came into the chapel one night that year and found it lit only by two candles. When her eyes became accustomed to the low light, she saw a woman in white rise from prayer in front of the church and float up, turning to show a desperately worried expression before vanishing. Could the ghost have known what was in store for Virginia? [32]

While Douglas was laying his groundwork to become president himself (it's widely held that all of his apparent friendliness toward slavery, despite being a Northerner himself, was simply a method to ingratiate himself to Southern voters), Abraham Lincoln was vying to take over Douglas's job as a United States Senator. In 1858, it was known that if the new Republican party could take control of the state legislature, Lincoln would be the man appointed to the Senate.

In the run-up to the local elections of 1858, when the Virginia ghost was said to have appeared, Douglas and Lincoln embarked on their famous series of debates, speaking before huge crowds in each of the seven Illinois cities they squared off in. Each side hired a stenographer, and their speeches were republished all over the country. They attracted no small amount of national attention (it was generally assumed that if Douglas held onto his job in the Senate, he'd be nominated for president by the Democrats in 1860), and many saw the whole exercise as a triumph of the American system—a series of substantive debates by expert speakers that could be read by people all over, and gave the constituents a chance to become better informed on the issues.

Again, people tend to downplay the role of slavery in these debates today, some claiming that the only issue they debated was whether slavery should be confined to the South, as Lincoln wanted, or allowed to expand based on popular votes in new territories, as Douglas did. But, in fact, the long debates covered a multitude of topics, including the basic idea of slavery in and of itself, and the idea that the nation could, in Lincoln's words, "permanently endure half slave and half free."

Lincoln made it clear throughout the debates that he was opposed to the very idea of slavery itself. However, he was not an "abolitionist," and stopped short of saying that the government should put an end to it. He believed that slavery was legal in the states where it already existed, and that the federal government had no right to change those laws. He could only hope that slavery would die out on its own if it was contained in the southern states, which he estimated would take about a hundred years. It's sometimes said today that Lincoln should have pushed for a plan in which the government would simply buy all the slaves and free them, which may have cost less than the war eventually did, but this ignores the fact that many slave owners never, ever would have agreed to this plan. Anyone who even suggested such a course of action would have been regarded as far too radical to be elected.

Douglas talked Lincoln into several corners during the debates by portraying him as anti-white, leading Lincoln to make a number of now-infamous statements that he had never claimed that blacks and whites were equal or that they should be allowed to intermarry. It's true that we can't possibly say that Lincoln was the most progressive guy in the world in terms of race; more liberal senators, such as Charles Sumner and Lyman Trumbull, were endlessly frustrated with Lincoln's middle-of-the-road stance on slavery. However, in fairness, it's worth noting that Lincoln made these statements while speaking to rural Illinois voters, who may have been against slavery (more or less), but weren't exactly against it due to any forward-thinking views on race. Laws restricting the rights of non-white people in Illinois tended to pass by huge margins, and these were the voters Lincoln needed to give his party control of the state legislature. He had to remain constantly on guard against charges that he was anti-white. Such is democracy—whatever Lincoln's private views were, he had to present the sort of public policy that voters would find acceptable. For his part, he said that rules about intermarriage and black rights should be local issues that each town and state should decide on their own, leading to a sly joke that if Douglas was so afraid of black rights, he had better come back to local government.

Still, whether he was backed into a corner or not, some of what Lincoln said in those debates (and in occasional letters and talks) do remind us that Lincoln wasn't perfect. Besides some badly outdated comments on race, one could fairly claim that the man was a lousy businessman, a distant and distracted father, and that he had a real knack for picking lousy generals to lead his army. (He had some pretty bad generals in charge before he got around to the more-effective Grant and Sherman, who, of course, still had issues of their own).

Still, Lincoln's stated views on race during the debates (and throughout his life) were not necessarily excusable, but they were politically savvy, and it could probably be argued of every bad thing Lincoln said or did, that if he hadn't said or done it, slavery would not have been brought to an end in 1865. It may very well not have happened if the war had been shorter or with anyone else in the White House.

In fact, the notion of actually ending slavery outright in 1858 seemed about as plausible as ending gun owner-ship outright seems today. People might get paranoid that it could happen, but even simple laws putting restrictions on gun sales are basically impossible to push through. The same was true of slavery then; even the weakest restriction was likely to be denounced as a radical intrusion on the rights of the slave states.

Rather than making strong statements about slavery at a time when it could have sparked a backlash that set the whole movement back, Lincoln played "the long game." Had Trumbull, Sumner, or one of the other anti-slavery hawks ever been elected president (which they almost certainly couldn't have been), they would probably not have been able to push the Thirteenth Amendment through Congress, as Lincoln ultimately did. Perhaps no one could have. And perhaps Lincoln even knew what he was playing for all along; in the handful of photographs of him in which he's smiling, one can imagine that there's a look about him as though he knows something other people don't.

If I sound like I'm on a bit of a rant here, it's because I am. Lincoln's views on race, slavery, and everything else are so widely misrepresented these days—by both the left and the right—that I often feel as though I need to defend his honor, even while I'm building up to examining the provenance of stories about him riding on a flying piano. And though there are certainly those who will say I'm exaggerating the role of slavery in the conflict between the states at the time, it's difficult to read newspapers of the day and come away with the impression that there was any other issue facing the nation at all. Slavery and the abolition movement were pretty much all they talked about in papers in those days when they spoke of the impending crisis.

But it's true that Lincoln was not an abolitionist, per se. Abolitionists were regarded as dangerous radicals who did more harm than good to the anti-slavery cause in those days, and some believed that simply ending slavery outright would do more harm than good for the people in bondage. After all, there were some four million slaves, few of whom had any education—what would become of them if slavery were ended all at once? Would they really be better off? By treating them as property and investments, wasn't it in the owners' best interest to keep them healthy, whereas the people hired to build the railroads and factories could be treated as disposable? To even suggest that there was an upside to slavery is indefensible today (and saying that employers had to own the employees in order to want to keep them alive is certainly no compliment to them), but all of these arguments made sense to many people at the time, even those who thought that slavery was an embarrassment, at best.

In this sort of world, it was Lincoln's middle-of-the-road view on how slavery should be handled that got him nominated for president in 1860, an event that may have only been possible in Chicago.

The 16th President

Lincoln helped the Republicans do well in the state elections in 1858 but not well enough to swing control of the state legislature over to the party, which kept him from getting Douglas's Senate seat. He ended up back in Springfield, practicing law with William Herndon and raising his children with Mary.

Still, the debates brought him a measure of national fame, and he became a popular speaker, traveling clear to the East Coast to give speeches. When 1860 came, bringing with it another presidential election, he was occasionally spoken of as a possible candidate.

The Democrats met for their own convention that year in Charleston, South Carolina, with no intention of renominating the sitting Democratic president, James Buchanan, and with everyone expecting the nomination to go to Douglas. But the slavery question had become so heated that it was splitting the Democratic party in two. After several ballots, Stephen Douglas had received more votes than everyone else every time, but never enough of a majority to officially secure the nomination. Southern delegates simply didn't think him pro-slavery enough; Lincoln had set something of a trap for him in the debates by getting him to say that if voters in the new territories could vote to allow slavery, they could also vote to outlaw it. That may seem like common sense, but saying so out loud was enough to make Douglas look like an enemy of the South in those days.

When no candidate had enough votes to be nominated after fifty-seven ballots (largely because the southern delegates had left in disgust, and there weren't enough votes still being cast for anyone to reach the requisite number), the party eventually gave up and closed the convention, reconvening six weeks later in Baltimore, where Douglas was quickly nominated. But the southern delegates who had "bolted" held another convention of their own, nominating Vice President John Breckinridge as their candidate, so there would be two Democratic candidates running for president that year, splitting the democratic vote.

Meanwhile, a third party had come into existence: an alliance of former members of the Whig and Know-Nothing parties, along with a few of the handful of southern democrats who opposed the idea of seceding from the Union, formed the Constitutional Union Party, which hoped to simply ignore the slavery question by taking no firm stance on it one way or the other. They nominated John Bell, a former Speaker of the House, Secretary of War, and senator, for president and Edward Everett for vice president (Everett would be remembered for giving a two-hour speech right before Lincoln's famously brief address at Gettysburg—few remember that he'd been a rival candidate in the election of 1860).

The Republicans, meanwhile, met in Chicago, with most observers expecting Sen. William Seward to be nominated.

But Seward's nomination was not the foregone conclusion some believed it to be; many voters feared that Seward's strong anti-slavery views made him unelectable. Behind the scenes, Lincoln's supporters had made a strong push among delegates to make Lincoln their second choice. One of Lincoln's supporters made the brilliant move of bringing in some actual rails that Lincoln himself had supposedly split thirty years before; the "western rail splitter who made good" image was critical at a time when slavery defenders were scoring points by claiming that the "wage slavery" and rampant unemployment of the North was an even worse system for menial laborers than slavery. Lincoln's story showed that the system worked: in a free society, citizens could improve their lot in life.

Though his actual time in Chicago had been limited, Illinois was Lincoln's home turf. He was promoted by the *Chicago Tribune* and the Republican Wigwam, and the stadium built just for the convention was packed with local supporters who promoted him so loudly that the sheer volume of their voices became the stuff of legend. This gave him just enough of an advantage to carry the day and win the nomination when it became clear that Seward didn't have enough support.

Lincoln was reasonably famous by then, but still obscure enough that many papers apparently still didn't even know if his name was "Abraham" or "Abram." Among the other candidates in the running, and compared to every previous president, Lincoln's resume makes him seem terribly out of place. Though we'd had one western log cabin-born president before (William Henry Harrison), Lincoln was not a former senator, governor, Founding Father, or war hero. He was just a guy who made good speeches and seemed to be in just the right place at just the right time, to a degree that one could practically call supernatural all by itself.

Lincoln's middle-of-the-road view on slavery was not regarded as middle-of-the-road in the South, though. Keeping slavery contained where it was meant blocking it from expanding into Mexico, South America, Central America, and Cuba (all of which the South had talked about bringing in as slave states, with varying degrees of seriousness, at times). With this policy, the South couldn't help but notice that it could soon be badly outnumbered in Congress, helpless to block new amendments if all of the non-slave states ganged up on them.

After all, this election showed that a man could be elected president without any approval from the South at all. Abner Doubleday, an officer stationed at Fort Sumter, off the coast of South Carolina, claimed that he was the only man in the vicinity who would admit to voting for Lincoln. (Doubleday never claimed to invent baseball, though his delightful memoir gives one the impression that he would have been glad to take credit for it.)

Lincoln received less than 40 percent of the popular vote nationwide. He got far more votes than any of the other three candidates, though; the Democrats were split, and the "old gentlemen" of the Constitutional Union Party, which barely had a delegate under sixty, didn't inspire nearly the enthusiasm that was seen among Lincoln's supporters. That's why 39 percent was enough to win the election handily that year. Lincoln won 180 of the 303 electoral votes and received a very comfortable 54 percent of the popular vote in free states.

But as soon as the election results were in, people began claiming to have dark premonitions about Lincoln's future.

He even appears to have had more than one of his own before he even arrived in Washington.

The Two Lincolns in the Mirror

In an 1885 letter, William Herndon spoke of Lincoln having strange presentiments and visions during his Springfield years. "He ... said to me more than once, 'Billy, I feel as if I shall meet with some terrible end.' He did not know what would strike him, nor when, nor where, nor how hard; he was a blind intellectual Sampson, struggling and fighting in the dark against the fates. I say on my own personal observation that he felt this for years."[33]

Maybe this was just Lincoln being depressed or fatalistic, but he does seem to have spoken about seeing visions and dreams that may have portended a dark fate.

According to a now-common tale, on the day of his election, Lincoln looked into a mirror in his Springfield home and saw something mysterious: two images of his face, one plain, and one faded. Legend has it that he took this as an omen that he would go on to win a second term (a feat no one had accomplished in a generation, since Andrew Jackson), but that he would not survive it.

While there's some debate over whether it was Abraham or Mary who saw the "vision" as a grim omen of the future, the story does seem to be true, in the main. Two different sources later spoke of the story—Noah Brooks, a journalist and friend of Lincoln repeated the story in 1865, and Ward Hill Lamon, Lincoln's bodyguard, told the story some years later.

By sheer merit of being published earlier, Noah Brooks's version of the story is probably the most reliable. His account was written just days after Lincoln's assassination and was published in the June 1865 issue of *Harper's*. According to Brooks, Lincoln had told him the story in November 1864, just after the general election. Brooks wrote that he had attempted to put down on paper the story "as nearly as possible in his (Lincoln's) own words."

This is how he quoted Lincoln:

It was just after my election in 1860, when the news had been coming in thick and fast all day, and there had been a great "Hurrah, boys!" so that I was well tired out, and went home to rest, throwing myself down on a lounge in my chamber.

Opposite where I lay was a bureau with a swinging-glass upon it (and here he got up and placed furniture to illustrate the position) and looking in that glass, I saw myself reflected, nearly at full length; but my face, I noticed, had two separate faces and distinct images, the tip of the nose of one being about three inches from the tip of the other. I was a little bothered, perhaps startled, and got up and looked in the glass, but the illusion vanished. On lying down again I saw it a second time—plainer, if possible, than before; and then I noticed that one of the faces was a little paler, say five shades, than the other.

I got up and the thing melted away, and I went off and, in the excitement of the hour, forgot all about it—nearly, but not quite, for the thing would once in a while come up, and give me a little pang, as though something uncomfortable had happened.

When I went home I told my wife about it, and a few days after I tried the experiment again, and (with a laugh) sure enough, the thing came again,

but I never succeeded in bringing the ghost back
after that, though I once tried very industriously
to show it to my wife, who was worried about it
somewhat. She thought it was "a sign" that I was
to be elected to a second term in office, and that
the paleness of one of the faces was an omen that
I should not see life through the last term.[34]

A quick reading here makes it look as though it wasn't so
much a "vision" as an optical illusion—created, perhaps, by
having the light from a nearby window hitting the mirror just
right or by the mirror simply being warped. But seeing as how
Mary's view of the case was exactly what happened—Lincoln
was re-elected, but didn't survive the second term—it's difficult not to view it as a grim portent of things to come.

Brooks wrote of the dream very shortly after Lincoln's
death, less than a year after he would have heard the story,
though close to five years after the actual event. He cautioned
against making too much of it, though: "The president, with
his usual good sense, saw nothing in all this but an optical
illusion," he wrote, "though the flavor of superstition which
hangs about every man's composition made him wish he had
never seen it. But there are people who will now believe that
this odd coincidence was 'a warning.'"

The other version of the mirror story comes from Ward
Hill Lamon, Lincoln's bodyguard. Lamon said that Lincoln
had told him the story just after he was nominated for a

second term (which would make it a few months before he would have told it to Brooks), though he didn't repeat the story until much later than Brooks did.

Lamon's version of the story is also worth repeating in full (with emphasis added to highlight the minor differences in the way it was told to Brooks). He had told a version of it in 1887; this version comes from his daughter's edited edition of his memories of Lincoln published in 1911:

> On the day of his renomination at Baltimore, Mr. Lincoln was engaged at the War Department in constant telegraphic communication with General Grant, who was then in front of Richmond. Throughout the day he seemed wholly unconscious that anything was going on at Baltimore in which his interests were in any way concerned. At luncheon time he went to the White House, swallowed a hasty lunch, and without entering his private office hurried back to the War Office. On his arrival at the War Department the first dispatch that was shown him announced the nomination of Andrew Johnson for Vice-President.
>
> "This is strange," said he, reflectively; "I thought it was usual to nominate the candidate for President first."
>
> His informant was astonished. "Mr. President," said he, "have you not heard of

your own renomination? It was telegraphed
to you at the White House two hours ago."

Mr. Lincoln had not seen the dispatch,
had made no inquiry about it, had not even
thought about it. On reflection, he attached
great importance to this singular occurrence. It
reminded him, he said, of an ominous incident
of mysterious character which occurred just after
his election in 1860. It was the double image of
himself in a looking-glass, which he saw while
lying on a lounge in his own chamber at
Springfield. There was Abraham Lincoln's
face reflecting the full glow of health and
hopeful life; and in the same mirror, at the
same moment of time, was the face of Abraham
Lincoln showing a ghostly paleness. On trying the
experiment at other times, as confirmatory tests,
the illusion reappeared, and then vanished as before.

Mr. Lincoln more than once told me that he
could not explain this phenomenon; that he had
tried to reproduce the double reflection at the
Executive Mansion, but without success; that it
had worried him not a little; and that the mystery
had its meaning, which was clear enough to him. To
his mind the illusion was a sign—the life-like image
betokening a safe passage through his first term as
President; the ghostly one, that death would overtake
him before the close of the second.[35]

The differences in the tellings are minor but significant—
in Brooks's version, it was Mary who saw the vision as a sign,
and in Lamon's, it was Abraham himself. This could perhaps
be chalked up to simply the minor ways Lincoln personally
changed the story around, depending on who he was telling the story to, or it could simply be down to the personal
prejudices and beliefs of Brooks and Lamon themselves and
how they wished to portray Lincoln. Lamon always said that
Lincoln believed in dreams. Brooks spoke of the president's
"good sense" about superstitions and said that it was Mary
who saw it as a sign (though, like many early biographers,
Brooks had little good to say about Mary).

Some still believe that the vision was a true omen whether
Lincoln actually believed that it was or not. Paranormal
author Hans Holzer even wrote that what had happened was
that Lincoln experienced a psychic phenomena in which "the
inner or true self has quickly slipped out...what the President saw was a brief out-of-the-body experience...which is
not an uncommon psychic experience."[36]

To me, the story always sounded simply as though Lincoln had seen an optical illusion in the mirror, not necessarily
a supernatural vision, perhaps caused by seeing in the mirror both his direct reflection and a reflection of a window in
which he was also being reflected. Notably, the effect could
be reproduced in the same mirror occasionally (though Lincoln wasn't around Springfield long enough after his election
to make too many attempts), but apparently not in other

mirrors, such as those at the White House. One can infer that the mirror had to be set up in just the right place, and positioned at just the right angle (it was specifically referred to as a "swinging" mirror) and, perhaps, that the light from the window had to be just right, as well.

In 2013, I arranged to tour the Lincoln home in Springfield, and arrived with a large mirror in hand to see if I could reproduce the effect. I was met by Susan Haake, the amiable curator of the Lincoln Home National Historic Site, who gave me a tour of the premises (including the outhouse—a three-holer) and helped to try to triangulate where the mirror might have been in 1860.

The exterior of Lincoln's home in Springfield, Illinois.
Courtesy Library of Congress.

Unfortunately, attempts to directly reproduce the effect by placing a mirror in just the right spot are not really possible. Exactly which room Lincoln would have been in at the time is difficult to determine (references to "my chamber" could be the bedroom or the living room or any number of places), and how the furniture was laid out in most of the rooms back in Lincoln's day isn't really known. A few rooms can be reproduced fairly well based on drawings that appeared in *Frank Leslie's Illustrated Newspaper*, but no record really exists of how most of the place was laid out in 1860. There is a chest of drawers belonging to Lincoln that was returned to the house in the 1970s, and some existing holes in it show that a swinging mirror could have been attached, but it isn't attached anymore, and exactly where the chest might have been in 1860 is anyone's guess (though the staff's guess is that it would have been in Lincoln's own bedroom. He and Mary were in separate rooms, as was common at the time.) Even carrying around a mirror of my own, though, I was unable to reproduce the effect.

So, exactly where the mirror was at the time is a mystery—as is the location of the mirror itself today, which disappeared from the record eventually. It's tempting to imagine that somewhere, someone has an antique mirror and has no idea that it once belonged to the Lincolns, and that it was in their mirror that Lincoln saw a vision of his future.

More Premonitions

Of course, this was probably not the only premonition of Lincoln's not surviving his presidency made just after the election. Lots of people claimed to predict his death, both based on psychic hunches and on more practical evidence, and continued to do so throughout his presidency.

That Lincoln himself suspected that he might not survive to see Springfield again can be seen in a line in his farewell address at the railroad depot in February 1861, as he journeyed off to assume the presidency: "Here I have lived a quarter of a century, and have passed from a young man to an old man. Here my children have been born, and one is buried. I now leave, not knowing when, or whether ever, I may return ... "

Lincoln probably didn't actually speak that line out loud. The version of the speech recorded by a reporter for the *Illinois State Journal* simply quotes the president-elect as saying, "Today I leave you," though toward the end of the speech he said, "With these few words I must leave you—for how long I know not."

But the quote about not knowing whether he would return was, without question, Lincoln's own, even if he didn't actually vocalize it that day. It comes from the "official" version of the speech, which Lincoln dictated to his secretary, John Nicolay, on the train as he traveled away (one can tell from the jerky and disjointed handwriting on the still-extant copy at the Library of Congress that it was copied down while the train was in motion). It may have been edited and revised a bit from the speech he actually gave, but the sentiment is certainly that of Lincoln himself. Whether he was feeling a presentiment that he might not survive or was simply being practical (it was the eve of his fifty-second birthday, and that a person under great mental strain may not live another eight years in those days wasn't an unreasonable guess), we can only speculate.

Perhaps the idea that he would never return to Illinois had been impressed on his mind after his final meeting with his stepmother, Sarah Bush Johnston-Lincoln, who supposedly had a premonition of her own that she would never see her stepson again upon his election.

According to Ward Hill Lamon's 1872 biography of Lincoln, shortly around February 1, 1861, roughly a week and a half before his journey to Washington, Lincoln went to visit his stepmother, in company with his cousin Dennis Hanks and one Col. Augustus Chapman (whose wife, Harriet, was granddaughter of Mrs. Lincoln). After some difficulty in crossing the icy Kickapoo River, they arrived at her home in Farmington, where "she fondled him as her own 'Abe' and he her as his own mother."

In the course of the visit, they stopped at the unmarked, "utterly neglected" spot where Lincoln's father was buried, and Lincoln began to make arrangements for a stone to be erected on the site (though Lincoln was never able to follow through on the plan; there was no memorial in place as of 1872, when the biography was written, and it remained unmarked until 1880).[37]

According to Lamon's retelling, when Lincoln parted from his stepmother for the last time, she would "never be permitted to see him again," for she felt that his enemies would assassinate him. He replied, 'No, no, mamma. They will not do that. Trust in the Lord, and all will be well: we will see each other again.'"[38]

Indeed, Lamon noted that fears of Lincoln's assassination, if not actual premonitions, were "shared by very many of his neighbors at Springfield; and the friendly warnings he received were as numerous as they were silly and gratuitous. Every conceivable precaution was suggested: some thought the (railroad) cars might be thrown from the track; some thought he would be surrounded and stabbed in some great crowd; others thought he might be shot from a housetop as he rode up Pennsylvania Avenue on inauguration day; and others still were sure he would be quietly poisoned long before the fourth of March (inauguration day). One gentleman insisted that he ought, in common prudence, to take his cook with him from Springfield—one from 'among his own female friends.'"[39]

William Herndon, the law partner and biographer, went to visit Mrs. Lincoln at her home in September 1865, only months after the assassination, to interview her. According to Herndon's notes on the interview (which reveal a number of odd capitalization choices), she said:

> I did not want Abe to run for Presdt—did not want
> him Elected—was afraid Somehow or other—felt
> it in my heart that Something would happen him
> and when he came down to see me after he was
> Elected Presdt I still felt that Something told me
> that Something would befall Abe and that I
> should see him no more.[40]

Again, this interview took place five years after the actual meeting took place, and a few months after the assassination, making it an "after the fact" premonition, but it was recorded very close after the event, and seems to have been backed up by people who probably were present and didn't have access to Herndon's notes. Of course, some have suggested that Mrs. Lincoln was a touch senile by this time (if only to explain why she gave away such priceless relics as young Lincoln's famous "sums book"), and at the end of the interview with Herndon, she apparently made a similar grim prediction about Herndon himself. According to his notes:

> When I was about to leave she arose—took me by
> the hand—wept—and bade me goodby—Saying I
> shall never see you again.[41]

So perhaps we have to take into account the possibility that saying "I will never see you again" may have just been something old Mrs. Lincoln did every time she said good-bye to anyone.

Herndon himself had spoken with Abraham Lincoln just before he journeyed to Washington, and Lincoln had promised that after his presidency they'd go on practicing law together as though nothing had ever happened, though he qualified the statement by adding, "If I live."[42]

Speaking at Independence Hall in Philadelphia en route to Washington, Lincoln made even further ominous statements. Speaking of the rift in the Union, he spoke of the words that had been adopted in that very hall in 1776, stating that the Declaration of Independence "was not the mere matter of the separation of the Colonies from the mother land, but...hope...which gave promise that in due time the weights should be lifted from the shoulders of all men, and that all should have an equal chance," and said that if the Union cannot be saved without upholding that principle, he "would rather be assassinated on this spot than to surrender to it."[43] It was an eerie line for people to remember a few years later.

As Lincoln traveled toward Washington, it was clear that there were dark days ahead for him, for his family, and for the United States of America, and no premonitions were necessary to know it. Fears that Lincoln was facing a danger of assassination in 1860 were not unfounded. Between his election and his journey to Washington, the states of South Carolina, Florida, Mississippi, Alabama, Louisiana, and Georgia had all seceded from the Union, and rumors of assassination attempts were rampant. He snuck into Washington on a train from Baltimore in secrecy (having secretly switched trains on the advice of detective Allan Pinkerton), disguised in an over-coat and a wide-brimmed hat, accompanied by Pinkerton and Ward Hill Lamon. There was no waiting crowd—only a single friend—to greet him when he arrived in the capital. "There was never a moment," Lamon wrote, "from the day he crossed the Maryland line, up to the time of his death, that he was not in danger of death by assassination."[44]

Of course, one shouldn't make too much of these pre-sentiments; Lincoln certainly didn't. He was making plans for reconstruction, the next step after the war, right up to the end of his presidency, and surprised many with a final speech expressing support for giving at least some of the freed slaves the vote (a sentiment that was regarded as quite radical at the time). And that the war would take a toll on him may not have been a presentiment so much as common sense.

Indeed, many of the predictions one can point to seem more rooted in people being honest about the cost of a war than in supernatural hunches.

Stephen Douglas, who was nearing the very end of his life by the end of the 1860 campaign, made a prediction of his own that later seemed like a prophecy. Visiting with Gen. Charles Stewart on New Year's Day 1861, he said, "Virginia, over yonder across the Potomac, will become a charnel-house...Washington will become a city of hospitals, the churches will be used for the sick and wounded. This house, the Minnesota block, will be devoted to that purpose before the end of the war."

He was right in every particular.[45] Indeed, he seemed to intuit more than others just how bad the war would be. He and Lincoln became closer in the early days of the Lincoln presidency, to the point that some spoke of him being brought into the cabinet. After the Confederates fired on Fort Sumter, officially turning the conflict violent, Lincoln drafted a call for 75,000 volunteers to fight. Douglas looked it over and said he suggested 200,000 instead.[46]

Douglas himself died only weeks later, worn to death by his own campaign, but apparently bearing no ill will to his old friend and rival. A couple of newspapers reported that he held Lincoln's hat for him at the inauguration. His efforts on behalf of the Union in the last months of his life don't excuse all of his politics, but they help his reputation a great deal, and, just like Lincoln, it could be said that even his mistakes had to happen, or the war that ended slavery might not have happened. It's easy to begin to see a grand design in these things sometimes.

Even Robert E. Lee, upon resigning from the United States Army to join the Confederacy, expressed sentiments like this. Lee didn't really believe that the southern states had the right to secede, and said that slavery was a moral and political evil (though he owned slaves himself). Like many who didn't care for slavery on principle at the time, he believed it was God's will, and would end when God willed it to. And right from the start, he saw grand designs in the war he fought not because he agreed with the politics, but to defend his home state of

Virginia. Though no one ever accused him of giving less than his best for the cause, he suggested that the bloody war might be God's punishment for slavery. In a May 1861 letter to a woman who had asked for his picture, days after rejecting an offer to command the Union army, Lee wrote that "Wherever the blame may be … I cannot raise my hand against my birthplace, my home, my children … I should like, above all things, that our difficulties might be peaceably arranged, and still trust that a merciful God, whom I know will not unnecessarily afflict us, may yet allay the fury for war. Whatever may be the result of the contest, I foresee that the country will have to pass through a terrible ordeal, a necessary expiation, perhaps, of our national sins."[47, 48]

Lincoln's Wartime Premonitions

Even months into his presidency, Lincoln spoke about premonitions of his own that he would not survive his days in the White House. In fact, he seems to have done so repeatedly throughout his time in office.

In 1862, Lincoln met Harriet Beecher Stowe, author of *Uncle Tom's Cabin*, at the White House. Her book about escaping slaves had galvanized the North and cut through the widely held belief that slaves were perfectly happy and content with their lot in life, and Lincoln supposedly greeted her by calling her "the little woman who wrote the book that started this great war." That particular quote didn't appear for years after the fact, and only came from second-hand sources, but in an 1864 article, Stowe herself wrote that Lincoln predicted his own death when she met him. According to Stowe, Lincoln told her that, "whichever way (the war) ends, I have the impression that I shan't last long after it's over."[49]

Francis Bicknell Carpenter's painting; it was during his period of work on it that he heard Lincoln mention his presentiment. Carpenter spent several months in the White House working on the painting; though people (then as now) criticized the proclamation as a sort of mealy-mouthed measure, Lincoln knew it would be part of his eventual legacy, a first major step toward the Thirteenth Amendment, which outlawed slavery officially. Courtesy Library of Congress.

This anecdote is particularly important. While Lincoln made several statements that sounded ominous in speeches, stories of him having actual premonitions of a grim fate were almost all first told in public after they had already come true. This one was published in early January 1864, when

Lincoln was still alive and well. The fact that one of them, at least, was published so early makes the various other stories about him saying things like this far more believable.

Lincoln seems to have made another such statement a few months after he met with Stowe. Francis Bicknell Carpenter, a painter, was introduced to Lincoln by Owen Lovejoy, a mutual friend, in February 1864, when he came to town to spend six months working on a painting of Lincoln's first reading of the Emancipation Proclamation to his cabinet. Carpenter said that Lincoln met Lovejoy, who was slowly dying, frequently during this time, and stated in an 1866 recollection that Lincoln once told Lovejoy: "This war is eating my life out; I have a strong impression that I shall not live to see the end."[50] If the quote is accurate, it would have been made in either February or March of 1864; Lovejoy died in Brooklyn on March 25.

Yet another such prediction would have been made only months later and was published only days after the assassination. Within a week after Lincoln died, a *Boston Journal* correspondent said that in July 1864, he'd told Lincoln once that he never doubted that the Union would triumph in the end, and Lincoln had replied with "Neither have I, but I may not live to see it. I feel a presentiment that I shall not outlast the rebellion. When it is over, my work will be done."[51]

As close as it comes to the event in question, though, we have to qualify this one a bit: it wasn't printed until after the fact, and could have just been the reporter promoting a common belief at the time that ending slavery was Lincoln's job, and that he had been killed because God needed someone who would be harder on the South to see the nation through reconstruction. Lincoln's "malice toward none, charity toward all" policies had plenty of opponents, even among his strongest supporters.

Lincoln is also sometimes quoted as saying that "I have a presentiment that God will call me to him through the hand of an assassin. Let his will, not mine, be done…So many plots have already been made against my life, that it is a real miracle that they have all failed, when we consider that the great majority of them were in the hands of skillful Roman Catholic murderers, evidently trained by Jesuits. But can we expect that God will make a perpetual miracle to save my life? I believe not."[52]

The last lines, in particular, are quoted now and then today. However, an examination of the source of the lines casts a lot of doubt on the entire quote's veracity. Lincoln was quoted as saying this in an 1886 book by Father Charles Chiniquy, a former priest who left the church and believed that the entire Civil War was part of the Catholic plot to take over the United States. In the book, *Fifty Years in the Church of Rome*, the quote appears as part of a very, very, long conversation with Lincoln that he purports to quote verbatim. The sheer length of the conversation, most of which is about Catholic conspiracies, would make it nearly impossible that Chiniquy could have remembered it all twenty minutes after it happened, let alone twenty years. Like many Lincoln biographers of the era, he wanted to make it perfectly clear that Lincoln agreed with all of his own philosophies and theories, no matter how far out they got.

Chiniquy would go on to claim that the eventual assassination in 1865 had been orchestrated by the Pope as revenge on Lincoln for having defended him (Chiniquy) in court in 1856. It takes a certain amount of arrogance to imagine that the Pope had a president assassinated because you had hired him once, and Chiniquy's surviving correspondence to Lincoln[53] doesn't give the impression that they were anywhere near as close as Chiniquy was claiming they had been by the 1880s.

Though Chiniquy's story doesn't seem to check out, that Lincoln was giving to predict his own death does seem well established. Whether these were really premonitions or Lincoln's own assessment of the war's toll on him is another matter. With constant news about casualties, it's easy to imagine how Lincoln would have had death on his mind.

Everyone else, did, after all.

And in such a world of death, the market was ripe for mediums, clairvoyants, and spiritualists.

Three

A World of Death: Growing Violence and the Rise of Spiritualism

hen the Civil War broke out, attempting to communicate with the dead had been a popular pastime for more than a decade. For some, "Spiritualism" had even become a religion.

Though people had claimed to have the ability to speak with the dead or to have first-hand knowledge of the afterlife, for ages, the beginning of the modern Spiritualist movement came in 1848 when Kate and Margaret Fox announced that they had contacted a spirit they initially called "Mister Splitfoot," who communicated with them by knocking on walls. Although Mr. Splitfoot was a name usually used for the devil, they later said he was the spirit of a person who had been murdered in the house and was now communicating through the girls.

The sisters began giving public seances demonstrating their ability to communicate with the dead, and soon "circles" in which participants would attempt to contact spirits were all the rage. Even among those who didn't join the spiritualist "religion," the belief that "mediums" could help you contact the dead became widespread and provided a measure of comfort for the bereaved. Even some who were not religious at all simply found the spiritualists' ideas more logical and scientific than the religious concepts they'd grown up with. Charles Hull, a Chicago real estate big shot, wrote in his diary that he was sure his late wife was still nearby; he didn't believe in a far-off heaven because "the distance is too great."[54]

Most often in the early days of seances, the "spirits" would make their presence known by rapping on tables or making objects float across the room. Sometimes they would take "control" over the medium, who would then speak in the spirit's voice. Other times they would control the medium by having them write things down. Very occasionally, they would even turn up visually. Though it was generally known that many "mediums" were frauds, the handful who were never caught red-handed still inspire believers today. Though Margaret Fox admitted in 1888 that she and her sisters had been faking the rapping sounds by cracking their joints, some believe she was lying (she did recant in 1889), and her confession did nothing to end the practice's popularity.

To put the widespread belief in the seances, even among educated people, in context, just consider what was happening with technology at the time. Electricity was still something people read about without actually seeing in action for themselves, but telegraphs could now send invisible messages across long distances. There were all sorts of new theories about mesmerism and such things that were presented as genuine science for a time. To open a newspaper and find that you could now communicate with the dead didn't seem too unreasonable, and even people who didn't attend seances tended to feel obligated to keep an open mind. Even "debunkers" such as Arthur Conan Doyle, who worked tirelessly to expose frauds, actually did believe in many of the principles of spiritualism, and worked to expose frauds only to weed out the fake mediums from among the real ones. Doyle, for the record, firmly believed the later stories that Abraham Lincoln once took a ride on a flying piano.

The press generally treated the practice with an amused detachment—when spiritualists held a convention in Chicago, the *Tribune* noted that there didn't seem to be very many spirit manifestations going on and slyly suggested that the spirits couldn't be bothered to pay the admission fee to the convention.

Spiritualism in Politics

On October 16, 1859, the *New York Herald* prepared an interesting notice for print: a statement that the *Spiritual Age* magazine was urging spiritualists throughout the country to vote for Gov. Nathaniel P. Tallmadge for president in the 1860 election in an effort to consolidate the power of spiritualism. Tallmadge, a former US Senator and current governor of the Wisconsin Territory, was a fan of spiritualism, and a reputed psychic, who wrote frequently about his encounters with spirits at seances, including the spirit of the late Vice President and Sen. John C. Calhoun. Calhoun's wild Beethoven-style haircut certainly made him look as though he would have made a terrific ghost; it's easy to imagine him rattling chains in an attic. (Perhaps the chains he insisted should bind others in life, as a major supporter of slavery, would be appropriate).

According to his letters, Tallmadge spoke to the spirit of Calhoun frequently, often in company with the Fox sisters themselves. Calhoun's spirit seemed to spend most of its time lifting tables and playing musical instruments, which were among the more common sights at seances of the day, and beating on tables "as if beating time to a march." And, as all talkative spirits of the nineteenth century seemed to, he spoke frequently about scripture. At one point, Tallmadge shut a pencil and piece of paper into a drawer, then opened it to find the words "I'm with you still" written on it.[55]

John Calhoun. With a haircut like this, it would be a shame if he wasn't haunting anything. Courtesy Library of Congress.

According to Tallmadge, several of Calhoun's friends had confirmed for him that it was the eight-years dead senator's handwriting, including the former governor of Calhoun's native South Carolina, and a few of them even noted that Calhoun was truly in the habit of writing "I'm" instead of "I am," (a peculiarity which impressed Tallmadge greatly).

Oddly, there wasn't much talk of politics when Calhoun's spirit was around. As a staunch proponent of the rights of slave-holding states in life, one would think Calhoun's spirit would have spoken some on the topic as a ghost in the late 1850s, when newspapers in his home state seemed only begrudgingly to print much of anything else. After all, the very day that the *Herald* was preparing the notice about spiritualists being urged to vote for Tallmadge in 1859, an abolitionist named John Brown was launching a raid on the Harper's Ferry armory.

Brown, who believed himself to be God's own agent on Earth, and whose opposition to slavery had grown violent, had arrived in Harper's Ferry, West Virginia, intending to lead a slave uprising. On October 16, 1859, he and eighteen of his followers led a raid on the local armory, intending to purloin the armory's stash of some 100,000 muskets to give to slaves. Though they succeeded in taking control of the armory itself, a local militia trapped them inside of it, eventually forcing them to retreat into a nearby engine house. Brown was eventually captured by a group of US Marines that included future Confederate general Robert E. Lee and was swiftly sentenced to be executed.

His hanging was attended by future Confederate general Stonewall Jackson, as well as John Wilkes Booth and Walt Whitman, who wrote about the event in a poem, "Year of Meteors 59–60," (which also touched on the 1860 meteor that some held up as a sign that the country would soon be split in two).

John Brown riding his own coffin to his hanging, as illustrated in Frank Leslie's Illustrated Newspaper *in 1859. Courtesy Library of Congress.*

It's particularly odd that attempts to contact Brown's spirit didn't become a mainstay of spiritual demonstrations, given that his execution galvanized both sides of the slavery debate (which hardly needed galvanizing). People who had once been moderate on slavery in the north started to become more and more sympathetic toward abolitionists, and anti-abolitionist paranoia spread like wildfire through the south. People still debate as to just how sane John Brown was (people who kill others because they believe themselves to be God's own agent on Earth are, as a rule, probably not entirely sane), but he was absolutely right—no amount of legislation would have brought about the end of slavery. His story was really only one of the many visible signs that the conflict between the North and the South was getting violent.

By the summer of 1860, abolitionists were being blamed for fires that raged across Texas (though more sensible heads noted that the recent heat wave and drought combined with the newly popular phosphorous matches were to blame), and at least one newspaper editor claimed that the arsonist attacks would soon be followed by slaves poisoning the drinking water. Vigilantes rounded up slaves and suspected abolitionists the same way their European ancestors rounded up suspected witches, torturing them into confessions before hanging them from lampposts, trees, and whatever else was handy. Though blacks got the worst of it, white Texans who had recently moved in from the North were killed as well. A supposedly abolitionist Methodist preacher's skin was displayed as a trophy, and children used his bones as toys.[56]

And all of this happened in the shadow of a presidential election. Lincoln's victory that fall was seen by many southern states as the last straw, despite the president-elect's repeated insistence that he had no intention of interfering with slavery in states where it already existed.

Only days after Lincoln was elected, South Carolina Gov. Francis Pickens gave a widely circulated address to the state congress urging the formation of a new southern nation, which included a suggestion of "the enactment of a law punishing summarily and severely, if not with death, any person that circulates incendiary documents, avows himself an abolitionist, or in any way attempts to create insubordination or insurrection among the slaves."[57] This, he believed, was for the abolitionists' own good, as it would at least protect them from "lynch law and illegal executions." His state officially seceded from the Union only days later, citing among its reasons Lincoln's own statements about slavery and "an increasing hostility on the part of non-slaveholding states."[58]

To be fair to the South, though Lincoln made every effort to assure them that he wasn't hostile to slavery in the states where it existed (to the frustration of radicals and abolitionists), this was the guy who'd been quoted as saying that the nation could not endure "half slave and half free." It was evident from his speeches that he hoped that slavery would die out, and simply keeping it contained would eventually endanger it, as the slave-holding states would soon be greatly outnumbered in Congress. And slavery formed the backbone of the South's economy.

Though it's commonly said now that the real reasons for secession were something to do with tariffs, fear of growing federal authority, or states' rights, the seceding states at the time were not at all ashamed to cite the protection (and eventual expansion) of slavery as the primary cause, and did so quite clearly. Other states that issued "articles of secession" in the coming months made frequent references to slavery (often in the first couple of sentences), and referred to Lincoln's party not as Republicans, but as "Lincoln Black Republicans." When the new Confederate constitution was drafted, there were few differences from the United States

Constitution, and very little that expanded or protected states' rights in any meaningful way. It could even by argued that, by giving their president a single six-year term (when no president in years had served more than four) and a line-item veto, they made the federal government a bit *more* powerful. The most obvious difference from the US Constitution was the explicit endorsement of, and protection for, slavery.

Of course, none of this means that it's entirely accurate simply to say that "the Civil War was about slavery." The desire to protect slavery led the South to secede, but to imply that Confederate soldiers were fighting to protect slavery themselves is a bit unfair; many were fighting to protect their homes from an army that was marching toward them. Very few of them owned slaves themselves. I tend to think of the Confederate soldiers as victims who were in the wrong place in the wrong era. Even many of the Confederate big shots weren't bad people at heart; they were products of their time who were on the wrong side of history.

And, though many northern soldiers were caught up in thinking of the South as "the land of slavery" and the North as "the land of the free," they were unduly flattering themselves. Laws restricting black rights in northern states tended to pass by huge margins. Though they sang "although they may be poor not a man shall be a slave" and "as he died to make men holy let us die to make men free," about the best you could say is that they were fighting for a peculiar sort of freedom. Even the most progressive northerners were generally products of their times, just like their southern counterparts.

As with any major conflict, there were good and bad people on both sides. Many southerners were against slavery, for reasons both good and bad (it seems odd that one could have a bad reason for it, but one southern diarist believed that being forced to sleep with their owners made slaves "fallen women" and thought it was degrading to have to live among such people. *Sheesh*). Some simply believed, not entirely unreasonably, that simply freeing millions of people who had no education into a world that wasn't exactly eager to hire them was only going to create a bigger mess.

Also, the official goal of the war, from Lincoln's point of view, was merely to bring the southern states back to the Union and end the "rebellion"—particularly in the early days after fighting broke out, when most believed that the war would be a very short dust-up. It could be argued that if the new Southern Confederacy had never fired on Fort Sumter, a federal fort off the coast of South Carolina, the war wouldn't have been waged at all, and Lincoln would have eventually been urged by the international community to simply let the South go.

In any case, few seriously imagined that the conflict could actually bring an end to slavery, though there are those who say that slavery was doomed when the first shot was fired on Fort Sumter. And they were right. Had the South not seceded, and had they not fired a shot, or even fought a shorter war, slavery might have endured decades longer than it did.

No one was killed in combat during the battle of Fort Sumter (though Abner Doubleday always believed that a few rebels were killed and buried in secret), reinforcing the widely held notion that the war would just be a dust-up, after which things would just go back to the way they were (or with the South as a separate nation, depending whose side you were on). But as the war progressed, more and more people came to realize that if the war didn't resolve the slavery question once and for all, we'd probably just end up fighting the war all over again in a few years. If the Union had just let the South go, they'd be fighting it over new territories soon.

John Brown was right that it would take blood to end slavery—the war that brought about that end turned out to be far bloodier than anyone could have conceived of in 1859, or even after the fighting first broke out. Battle after battle, in which tens of thousands engaged in combat, ended with 30 percent casualty rates. It's sometimes been noted that nearly every Civil War battlefield, hospital, prison, and graveyard is said to be haunted today. Whether one believes in ghosts or simply thinks that ghost stories are part of how we process death as a society, it's a small wonder. Blood was shed on American soil at rates never imagined before.

After the Battle of Shiloh alone, in April of 1862, there were more than 20,000 soldiers dead, wounded, maimed, or missing. People heard the cannons for miles around. During the night, soldiers would try to sleep as the screams of the wounded and dying cut through the sound of the rain sloshing in the mud and the blood. This was only the first of the major battles. There were dozens more to come, each bringing thousands of fatalities.

And those were just the deaths in battles—soldiers were far more likely to die of disease than in combat.

By the end of the war, the number of dead soldiers would be in the hundreds of thousands—today's estimates of the total number of mortalities tend to hover in the range of 600,000 (counting the Confederates), though they sometimes stretch far higher. The war affected nearly every household.

The soldiers grew used to the deaths. Elisha Hunt Rhodes, a Union soldier who had lost his own father a few years earlier, wrote to his family that "Death is so common that little sentiment is wasted. It is not like death at home."[59]

Death at home, though, was still a matter attended to with great ceremony, and more than a little superstition. Some of the soldiers' Victorian families still covered the mirrors in the house if there was a corpse in the home, and when someone died in the house it was customary to stop the clocks to avoid bad luck (which may have evolved into the urban legend that clocks were often displayed in stores with the hands set at a certain position—the time when Lincoln was shot. (See chapter 7.)

Cities had only recently begun creating "garden cemeteries" for the dead, rather than burying them in small family plots or churchyards. Lincoln himself, visiting Chicago after his election and holding a meeting at Ebenezer Peck's north-side mansion, could have looked out of the top-floor window of the mansion to see Chicago's City Cemetery, which was, like many garden cemeteries, a popular picnic spot.

He could hardly imagine, looking out at the graveyard, that the grounds would soon contain the graves of countless soldiers, including thousands of Confederate prisoners of war (or that within a decade it would be converted to a park named in his honor), though if a story were found saying that he went downstairs from the top floor and told everyone that he'd had a strange vision of soldiers' graves filling the ground as far as the eye could see, it wouldn't seem like an anomaly at all. Whether you blame psychic powers or intellect, Lincoln often seemed to be able to see a few steps further into the future than everyone else around him. He was not, as we've seen, above telling people about premonitions, either.

Wartime Spiritualism

With the Civil War becoming ever bloodier as the 1860s progressed, the market for people who wanted to communicate with a departed loved one skyrocketed. Indeed, it's sometimes said that spiritualism had two major bursts of popularity in the United States—during the Civil War, and during World War I (after which so many frauds had been exposed that it never quite regained its earlier foothold). The Civil War brought on carnage that no one was prepared for, and the idea that they could still communicate with the lost soldiers brought many people a measure of comfort, even to those who remained skeptical that the messages they received were genuine.

The *Banner of Light*, a spiritualist newspaper, contained a whole section of messages from spirits, and messages from fallen soldiers were fairly common. Surprisingly, not all of the messages were particularly comforting. The "Message Department" section of the April 1865 issue contained a missive from John N. Hanley of the Seventy-Second New York, who said he was captured at Gettysburg and died in a rebel prison in Georgia.[60] "I've not been in a very pleasant mood since I went out of this world," he said, since his family didn't know what had happened, and the man he'd paid in advance to send his effects to his family had pocketed the money and never held up his end. Another message came from John Murphy, who had been in "Spirit Land" since May, and was a little down, because Spirit Land wasn't quite what he'd expected, and he was afraid to tell his parents that after his experiences there, he was no longer a Catholic.[61]

The Lincolns, too, experienced a death in the family during the war.

In February 1862, a year after arriving in Washington, their two youngest surviving sons, Tad and Willie, both became ill (another son, Thomas, had died in Springfield, and their eldest, Robert, was off at Harvard). Tad eventually recovered, but poor Willie died at the age of eleven on February 20.

Willie Lincoln, whose ghost is occasionally said to have been seen around the White House in the late nineteenth century, and whose spirit Mary Lincoln is known beyond doubt to have tried to contact. Courtesy Library of Congress.

Mary was inconsolable, too hysterical to give any comfort to Tad or to attend the funeral services held in the White House. She wasn't seen in public for several weeks. Abraham himself was seen pacing the floor of his office, saying, "This is the hardest trial of my life! Why is it? Why is it?"

Willie's body was embalmed and interred, temporarily, in the family vault of William Thomas Carroll, clerk of the Supreme Court. (It was assumed that the remains would eventually be taken back to Illinois and re-interred, as indeed they were). Lincoln allegedly had the coffin removed twice in the next few years to look upon Willie's face again, unable to bear the thought of leaving him alone in the cold, dark tomb.

Lincoln himself later asked a Union officer, "Do you ever find yourself talking with the dead?" Before the office could reply, Lincoln went on with, "Since Willie's death, I catch myself every day involuntarily talking with him, as if he were with me."[62]

He probably did not mean this entirely literally, but stories of Willie's ghost haunting the White House are not unheard of. A widely printed 1973 newspaper article stated that a ghostly child, thought to be William Lincoln, had been glimpsed around the White House (though the article didn't give any specific sightings).[63] Various sources claim that the ghost was seen during the Grant and Taft administrations. An 1873 biography of medium Fannie Conant said that Willie Lincoln spoke through her frequently in the early

1860s, correctly predicting his father's re-election and death at the hands of an assassin.[64]

Though historians differ as to whether Abraham Lincoln ever actively sought comfort for Willie's death or advice in war matters from spiritualists, it's almost universally agreed that his wife did, and evidence to back it up is practically unimpeachable. Certainly, her grief at Willie's death was immense, to a point that people feared for her sanity. Just how many seances she attended isn't really known, but strong evidence connects her to at least a few of them, and Abraham may have joined her now and again. Some suggest he did it for entertainment, some said he went along to make sure some charlatan wasn't conning Mary out of all their money, but others think he was willing to take a chance and try to reach out to spirits for advice on the war.

And, yes, he may have even taken a ride on a flying piano.

The Colchester Case

According to Noah Brooks, Mary was induced to try spiritualism by a "seamstress employed at the White House," usually said to be Elizabeth Keckley, a former slave who had bought her own freedom some years before and taken up work as a dressmaker in Washington. In 1860, Keckley even worked for Jefferson Davis's wife, who tried to convince her to come to Richmond upon the secession (fully confident, according to Keckley, that within a few months the war would be over and she would be living in the White House as First Lady), but she stayed in Washington and became Mrs. Lincoln's employee, friend, and confidante.

As Brooks put it, "A seamstress at the White House induced Mrs. Lincoln to listen to the artful tales of a so-called spiritual medium who masqueraded under the name of Colchester, and who pretended to be the illegitimate son of an English duke. The poor lady at the time was well-nigh distraught with grief at the death of her son Willie. By playing on her motherly sorrow, Colchester actually succeeded (in) inducing Mrs. Lincoln to receive him at the Soldier's Home."[65]

"Pretended" is the operative word in the description of Lord Charles Colchester. He was, by all accounts, not really a medium or the son of a duke. But Mary Lincoln was far from the only prominent person he tricked; he was briefly a minor celebrity in Washington.

In Brooks's account, Mary met him at the Soldier's Home, where "in a darkened room, he pretended to produce messages from the dead boy by means of scratches on the wainscoting and taps on the walls and furniture." Mary excitedly told Brooks about the encounter and asked him to attend a subsequent seance in the White House itself.

Brooks declined the offer, so we'll never know what went on at Colchester's White House seance (if, indeed, it ever took place), but Brooks took the chance to see a Colchester "sitting" in the home of a Washington gentleman (which cost him a dollar—why he paid for this "sitting" instead of attending one for free is anyone's guess, though one can imagine that perhaps he simply didn't want to be at the same sitting as Mrs. Lincoln, which may have been terribly awkward to witness).

During the seance, it appeared as though drums were playing on their own accord in the darkened room as Colchester and the guests sat holding hands around a table, but Brooks reached out into the darkness and grabbed "a very solid and fleshy hand that held a bell that was being thumped on a drumhead." By the time his friend had lit a match, Brooks had been attacked with a cymbal, and the light came on to show his face covered in blood as he grasped Colchester by the wrist.

Colchester fled the scene, but apparently went straight to the White House, where he told Mrs. Lincoln that if she didn't get him a pass to New York from the War Department (required for travel out of Washington at the time), "he might have some unpleasant things to say to her." Mary and Brooks arranged to have him return to the White House, where Brooks himself confronted Colchester, showing him his scarred forehead and saying, "You know that I know you are a swindler and a humbug. Get out of this house and out of this city at once."

Brooks wrote that he never saw or heard of Colchester again, but Colchester in fact made the news once more in August 1865, when his act of making objects appear to float around the room got him brought into court on charges of (get this) "juggling without a license." Ulysses S. Grant was listed as a witness against him; the nature of Grant's dealings with Colchester are not known, but twenty years later, interestingly enough, Grant responded to rumors that he had become a spiritualist himself by saying that "although he had never attended a seance in his life, he believed spiritualism to be a system of jugglery carried on by jugglers."[66]

Mary's reaction to hearing that Colchester was a charlatan does not seem to be recorded (I would imagine that she would have been devastated, had she believed the accusations), but her meeting with Colchester was certainly not her only meeting with spiritualists during her time as First Lady.

Spiritual Advice for the President

Though Mary's interest in seances is well documented, whether President Lincoln himself was ever involved is a matter of some debate—and has been since he was still alive. The press printed many rumors of him attending seances, but most were nothing but fiction and innuendo.

We do know that Lincoln was certainly offered a lot of spiritual *advice*. The Lincoln Papers in the Library of Congress include one letter from a medium that begins, "I am your heavenly father" before descending into four pages of rambles. In December 1861, medium J. B. Conklin mailed in some written communications from the spirit of Edward Baker, who had died two months previously (and whose "message," written in backwards handwriting, began, appropriately enough, with, "You will no doubt be surprised to receive this from me . . . ").[67]

In 1874, a story circulated that Lincoln had (perhaps unwittingly) ordered the release of Sioux Chief Big Eagle, who had been held in Davenport for his participation in the Dakota War of 1862, on the advice of spirits.

According to the story,[68] a seance was held at the home of Mrs. Fannie Conant, a Boston resident, in the fall of 1863, around the same time she was allegedly getting messages from Willie Lincoln. A message was received from Little Crow, a Sioux leader who had been killed in Minnesota in 1862, claiming that the release of Big Eagle, then being held at Davenport, Iowa, "would tend to strengthen the peace between the Sioux Indians and the whites." A reporter wrote that "Little Crow's message was strengthened by a message from the spirit of little Willie Lincoln, son of Mr. Lincoln, who had died not long before, and who 'manifested' that he believed that great good would result from the liberation of Big Eagle."

The 1874 article states that one of those present at the seance was Davenport lawyer George S. C. Dow, who wrote to Mrs. Lincoln, who was then so deeply moved by the message that she arranged for Dow to meet the president, and that the release was ordered in late 1864 via Special Order No. 430.[69]

A great deal of this is actually verifiable, though the spiritualist angle is difficult to prove, as it wasn't told until a decade after the fact. Big Eagle really was confined in Davenport and really was released by special order. There are two letters from Dow to Lincoln regarding Big Eagle in the Library of Congress's Lincoln Papers, the last of which is dated just about two weeks before the order was given. From the letters, it appears that Lincoln did give the order for release upon a personal meeting with Dow, though the order failed, at the time, to actually bring about the release—the officer at Davenport seems to have thought the order, written in pencil, was bogus. A proper military order was needed, and eventually given. However, no mention of the spirit message is made in the letters,[70] or in Big Eagle's own account of the battle and his imprisonment (though it doesn't mention his release at all).[71]

The actual release order sold at auction in 1999 for just over $6,000.

The Shockle Seance

Lincoln's 1864 decision to ask for Big Eagle's release may not have come from any spiritual message, real or imagined, but stories that he was taking advice from the dead were fairly common by then. In April 1863, the *Boston Saturday Evening Gazette* published a lurid account of spiritualism at the White House that ended up being reprinted in papers all over the country (including, of course, the gleeful *Chicago Times*, the former Stephen Douglas organ, which delighted in thinking that Lincoln was getting spiritual advice from the ghost of their old champion).

According to the article, some time around the night of April 20, 1863, the president had given a "spiritual soiree" in the Crimson Room at which Mrs. Lincoln, Gideon Welles (Secretary of the Navy), Edwin Stanton (Secretary of War), and a couple of other notables were invited to test the powers of a medium known as Mr. Charles E. Shockle.[72]

According to the reporter, one Mr. Melton,[73] the group was seated around the table at around eight p.m. The president was immediately called away on some urgent business, and the spirits gave evidence of their displeasure with him having better things to do than confer with them by pinching Stanton's ears. Things didn't calm down until some time after Lincoln returned (and after he'd had a hearty laugh at his secretaries getting their hair pulled by spirits).

After an hour or so of pictures swaying on the walls and the candelabra floating toward the ceiling, Shockle was "fully under spiritual influence," and announced to the president that an "Indian" spirit had arrived and wished to chat.

"Well, sir," Lincoln was quoted as saying, "I should be happy to hear what his Indian majesty has to say. We have recently had a visitation from our red brethren, and it was the only delegation, black, white, or blue, which did not volunteer some advice about the conduct of the war."

A pencil and paper were hidden beneath a napkin, and when the napkin was removed seconds later (less time than it has required me to write this) the paper was filled with aphorisms such as, "Haste makes waste, but delays cause vexation." The note was signed "HENRY KNOX."

"This is not Indian talk, Mr. Shockle," said the president. "Who is Henry Knox?"

Here is the first obvious sign that something is amiss with the story—Lincoln surely would have known that Henry Knox was the first secretary of war. Having been informed of this, according to the article, Lincoln asked General Knox "if it is within the scope of his ability to tell us when this rebellion will be put down."

Again, the piece of paper was hidden, and invisible hands wrote on it that "Washington, Lafayette, Franklin, Wilberforce, Napoleon, and myself have held frequent consultations upon this point ... Lafayette thinks the rebellion will die of itself; Franklin sees the end approaching, as the South must give up for want of the mechanical ability to compete against Northern mechanics. Wilberforce sees hope only in a negro army."

At this point in the seance, the mirror on the wall became illuminated with a picture of the *Alabama*, a Confederate commerce raider—basically a legalized pirate ship—that Lincoln was hoping to capture, and which was, at the time, wreaking havoc on Union merchant ships off the coast of Brazil. In the picture in the mirror, the ship was seen unmanned, a veritable ghost ship, under the shadow of an English fort. The picture vanished and was replaced by purple lettering saying, "The English People demanded this of England's aristocracy."

Lincoln astutely viewed it with suspicion. "So England is to seize the *Alabama* finally? It may be possible, but, Mr. Welles, don't let one gunboat or monitor less be built."

The president, in Melton's account, then expressed a sentiment that only the pictures had made him think anything "heavenly" was happening, and asked for the advice of Stephen Douglas. Shockle said he would try to get him, but noted that sometimes he didn't have control over which spirit sent messages (hence the fact that the "Indian" spirit had turned out to be the very white Henry Knox).

Shockle then paused, stood up, and spoke in a voice that, according to Melton, anyone who had ever heard Douglas speak would recognize as the senator's own, urging the president to stay the course and fight on, and to follow any victories with "energetic action."

"I believe that," Lincoln said, "whether it comes from spirit or human."

At this point, the party broke up, with Shockle "much prostrated."

The story doesn't seem to indicate any great belief in spiritualism on Lincoln's part, as he maintains skepticism throughout (and one can assume that if he truly believed it was more than simply entertainment, he would have asked after the spirit of Willie). Even if the article did show Lincoln genuinely seeking ghostly advice, it could hardly be held up as evidence that Lincoln held any regard for the practice. But the article was almost certainly pure fiction. Gideon Welles didn't say anything about the seance in is diary, and neither Lincoln nor any of the other mentioned guests had ever referred to it though, considering that the story was printed in many papers both in the North and South, it's notable that they don't seem to have denied it, either.

More to the point, Charles Shockle's appearance in this article is about the only mention of a medium by that name that anyone has ever found. As near as can be told, the man didn't exist. A medium famous enough to get an invitation to the White House would presumably have been mentioned in the press elsewhere as a lecturer or something, but his name comes up nowhere else.

Even Mr. Melton himself may have been a fictional character, and the *Gazette* did nothing to support him; a June issue buried a retraction among other small news items on the second page, stating, "'By authority' the alleged spiritual seance at the White House has been pronounced a humbug. General Knox did not give Secretary Stanton any hard raps and Secretary Welles's beard was not pulled by spiritual agency."[74] Two weeks later, the spiritualist journal *Banner of Light* ran a letter stating in no uncertain terms that the story was fiction.[75]

The *Banner of Light*, though, wasn't above publishing articles saying that Confederate President Jefferson Davis was asking for spirit advice too; one of their messages from an 1865 issue purportedly came from former President Zachary S. Taylor, responding to questions from Jefferson Davis, who happened to be his son-in-law. "Well, President Davis," the spirit said, "You ask, 'Will I be successful in my present undertaking?' and I answer 'No!' Why, man, are you a fool? Can you not see which way you are drifting?"[76] *The Banner* provided no evidence that Davis was actually seeking spirit advice beyond the quote from the medium channeling Taylor who said so. By the time it went to press, the war was over. Davis was captured three days before the issue was published.[77]

It's worth noting, though, that just after the Shockle story went to press with its tale of Wilberforce's spirit pushing for a negro army, the Battle of Milliken's Bend broke out in Mississippi. This was the first battle in which large numbers of black soldiers played a major part in fighting for the Union, and, though having black soldiers fighting was highly controversial in the Union before, after their valuable contribution in Milliken's Bend, the debate was effectively over. The rise of black soldiers did give the Union a major advantage over the Confederacy, which continued not to allow black soldiers until the very tail end of the war, when it started conscripting slaves in desperation. (The idea that there were large numbers of active black Confederate soldiers is a persistent myth today; armed black people was the last thing the southern states wanted.) The role black soldiers played in bringing the Union around to the idea of abolishing slavery cannot be overstated.

However, not all of the predictions made by the spirits came to pass. The *Alabama* would be sunk a year later by the Union warship *Kearsage* off the coast of France in the Battle of Cherbourg, not by the English.

Far more papers ran the story of the seance than ran the later retraction (the spiritualist *Banner of Light* actually seemed far less inclined to believe it than the major papers), and the image of the president attending seances stuck in the public mind. But it wasn't until more than a decade after his death that stories began to circulate of the president attending a seance where he floated on a piano.

Four

Lincoln's Piano Ride

I like to imagine that the stories of Lincoln riding a flying piano are true, if only because so many stories of Lincoln portray him in Washington as desperately unhappy. It's nice to imagine a scene where he's having fun. Sometimes I picture him just sitting there on an old upright, bouncing as the piano rose and fell to the rhythm of the jaunty tune being played on it by a medium, grinning like a kid riding one of those rocket-ship rides they used to have outside of the Kmart in my hometown. Other times, I let my imagination run wild and picture him zooming into Richmond on the back of a flying baby grand shouting "Yeeee-ha!" and waving his stovepipe hat in the wind, ready to sail right into Jeff Davis's office for a round of good old-fashioned fisticuffs, aided, perhaps, by a bunch of animated utensils. Perhaps a fireplace poker could whiz through the air and depants the Confederate president.

The latter image comes strictly from my own imagination, of course, but the former, of Lincoln riding on a piano as it levitated up and down from the floor, is a part of Lincoln folklore and is backed up by at least one supposed witness and occasionally taken seriously by historians. Doris Kearns Goodwin relates the story as a matter of fact in her Pulitzer Prize-winning *Team of Rivals.*

Abraham Lincoln, joined by S. P. Kase, sits on a piano while Belle Miller, a spirit medium, plays a march that causes it to rise up and down. Did this ever happen?[78] Courtesy author's collection.

It's certainly not out of the question that Lincoln might have been invited to hop on a floating piano once or twice. Lots of people were back then. Watching objects float about the room, apparently lifted by spirits, was a popular pastime in the 1860s, and Mrs. Lincoln, at least, is known to have visited a house where just such a thing was known to happen. The story eventually spread that Abraham had followed Mary to a seance at the home of Mr. and Mrs. Laurie in Georgetown, where a medium (their daughter, Mrs. Belle Miller) made a piano float, with Lincoln sitting on it.

Though the facts of the story can't all be verified, quite a few of them actually can.

On January 1, 1863, Sen. Orville Browning of Illinois, who was named to the Senate to fill the seat vacated by the death of Stephen A. Douglas, wrote in his diary that Mrs. Lincoln had asked him to go riding with her (at "2½ pm"), and told him during the carriage ride that "she had been, the night before, with old Isaac Newton," (a friend of the family and sitting commissioner of agriculture), out to Georgetown to see a Mrs. Laurie, a spiritualist, and she made wonderful revelations to her about her little son Willie, who died last winter, and also about things on the Earth. Among other things, she revealed that the cabinet were all enemies of the president, working for themselves, and that they would have to be dismissed, and others called to his aid, before he had success."[79]

At this point in his diary, Browning was given to speaking ill of the cabinet himself. January 1, 1863, was the day that the Emancipation Proclamation went into effect, and Browning felt that it would serve only to fan the hatred in the South while dividing the North, and that the cabinet should never have let Lincoln issue it. Immediately after the ride, he spoke with a "Mr. Ewing" who feared that 100,000 Union soldiers would lay down their arms over it. The next day, Browning spoke with Secretary of State William Seward about the Proclamation (after a pleasant game of whist with Seward and his wife), and Seward, who Browning judged as an "ultra abolitionist," expressed the opinion that the rebellion could not be crushed without also crushing slavery.

And here we have a fascinating document about how the war's relationship to slavery evolved over time. Though everyone knew that the South had left the Union to protect slavery, the war was thought of, at least at first, as a war to crush the rebellion and save the Union, not a war to end slavery. Saying that it was a slavery war would have jeopardized the loyalty of the border states by showing that the southern states were right that they had to secede in order to protect their property. However, over the course of the first eighteen months of the conflict, when the war was looking less like a short dust-up, people began to realize that if it didn't settle the question of slavery once and for all, it would probably just happen all over again—and soon. In 1862, Lincoln had been floating ideas such as colonizing freed slaves in Central America, though whether this speaks to a rather unprogressive view of equality on his part, a willingness to explore all options in a tough situation, or an attempt to make the coming Emancipation Proclamation easier to swallow depends a great deal on what the source you're reading thinks of Lincoln to begin with.

When it was issued, the Emancipation Proclamation didn't end slavery outright—it only dealt with slaves in territories the Union captured from that day on, which was about as much as Lincoln thought he could get away with at the time. But it made ending slavery a formal goal of the war and gave the Union access to countless newly freed slaves, making it a canny military move (not to mention that casting the war as a battle against slavery made it even less likely that the French or English would join in on the Confederacy's side). Crucially, it wasn't a drastic enough measure to scare the border states out of the Union, which was always a delicate balancing act, but it was still controversial in the North, just as Browning thought it would be. Wilbur F. Storey at the *Chicago Times*, exhibiting less power as a prophet than he had with the Meteor of 1860, confidently predicted that the proclamation would "be known in history as the most wicked, atrocious, and revolting deed recorded in the annals of civilization."[80] Months later, Storey would become a Civil War trivia footnote when he described the Gettysburg Address as "silly, flat, dishwatery utterances."

Read a few editorials like the kind Storey wrote and you'll see why Lincoln wasn't willing to go further than he did (and why Lincoln might have been willing to get counsel from anyone who had good advice to give, up to and including the dead). Orville Browning had no trouble finding other highly placed officials who agreed with his assessment that the move would only cause disunion at a time when unity of purpose was of the utmost importance.

Browning, for his part, had been to a seance or two in his day. An entry from his diary from 1853 has an account of attending a seance where he observed some of the usual tricks of spirit rapping and table tipping. "I am utterly satisfied," he wrote, "that there was no trick or collusion about the matter, and whilst I discard all belief and the presence and agency of the spirits of the departed, I confess myself utterly unable to account for the phenomenon."[81] However, he wasn't always impressed. In 1855, he went to hear a spiritualist give a lecture and described her talk as "intolerable twaddle (and) incomprehensible nonsense."

Besides being a fascinating document of the life and minds of Lincoln's family, his cabinet, and their friends at such a critical juncture in history, the early January 1863 entries in Browning's diary are perhaps the strongest contemporary evidence in existence that Mrs. Lincoln was, indeed, actively consulting spiritualists for both personal and political matters, since most of the rest is from second-hand sources, guesswork, and accounts that might have been invented years later only to make Mrs. Lincoln look bad.

It is also key evidence that Abraham may, in fact, have taken a ride on a piano during a seance.

The "piano ride" is usually said to have happened in the home of Mrs. Laurie, whose daughter, then known as Mrs. Belle Miller, has been said to have performed the trick of making pianos levitate elsewhere. In fact, from other accounts of her, it appears that it was her most popular trick. If we're to establish that Lincoln might have really taken that ride, the fact that we can conclusively show that Mrs. Lincoln met with Mrs. Laurie is critical.

The Lauries

Cranston and Margaret Laurie were Washington natives who married in 1830; their eldest daughter, Belle, was the reputed piano-playing medium. The Lauries were, in fact, devoted spiritualists, specializing in creating "spirit art" that was much admired by one Emma Hardinge, who wrote about them in the 1871 *Year-Book for Spiritualism*. Belle married James Miller, a friend of the Lincolns, which lends some credibility to the idea that Abraham would have come to their house at one point or another.

Belle Laurie-Miller's piano-levitating tricks were witnessed and documented by several sources over the years.

One William Henry Chaney (who is sometimes said to be the father of author Jack London, though he denied it) told a story about Mrs. Miller in an 1874 issue of *Common Sense: A Journal of Live Ideas*. He said that he had met the Lauries in 1866 (a year after Lincoln died) and once asked Belle to show her piano-tilting trick in the parlor of a grand hotel. Belle demurred, saying she wasn't good enough to play in front of so many superior pianists, but invited him out to the house in Georgetown, where she was more confident of her abilities. Chaney astutely pointed out that this looked suspicious— skeptics were sure to hold it up as proof that the home piano was mechanically rigged to appear to float. She consented to play the hotel piano and, according to Chaney, it dutifully tipped up and down in time to the march she played on it.[82]

Chaney said that Mrs. Laurie claimed that Belle had done seances for Mr. Lincoln several times so that he could consult the spirits of Thomas Jefferson, Benjamin Franklin, and George Washington, and said that the spirit who physically tipped the piano around while Belle played it was a dead soldier who had died "in defense of the old flag," and that President Lincoln had very much enjoyed watching the piano rise and fall, and saw the spectacle on many occasions (though he stops short of saying he rode it).

Chaney also claimed that he had seen several notes in Abraham Lincoln's handwriting inviting Belle to come to the White House for seances. These, he said, were kept in secrecy (and have never emerged). However, he also once told a story of Margaret Laurie arguing for the release of a soldier who had been wrongfully arrested as a deserter,[83] and a letter from Laurie to Lincoln preserved at the Library of Congress backs this portion of the story up. That he knew about the deserter letter at all makes him a fairly good source, even though the letter in question doesn't mention spiritual matters.[84]

Chaney was only a second-hand source as to Lincoln's seances with the Millers, but J. C. Laurie, Belle's brother, gave a first-hand account in 1885. He wrote that "I have on several occasions seen Mr. Lincoln at a circle at my father's house... and I have heard him make remarks while in that condition, in which he spoke of his deceased son Willie, and said that he saw him. I have on several occasions seen Mr. Lincoln take notes of what was said by mediums. At one circle, I remember that a heavy table was being raised and caused to dance about the room by what purported to be spirits. Mr. Lincoln laughed heartily and said to my father, 'Never mind, Cranston, if they break the table, I will give you a new one.'"[85] The letter, published in a religious magazine, attracted a reply from William Herndon, who stated that he knew nothing of Lincoln's belief (or disbelief) in spiritualism, though he had reason to believe that the future president had attended a seance or two in Springfield, if only out of curiosity. It should also be noted that the story was told more than twenty years after the fact, which damages its pedigree a bit.

Still, we can establish that Mrs. Lincoln went to seances at the Lauries' house, and that this was the sort of place where you might see a piano float. We can also establish that there's at least a chance that President Lincoln himself may have attended a seance now and then, with at least one witness saying that he was at the Lauries', and one second-hand source saying that he'd seen the piano float.

As to the ride itself, there are two first-hand witnesses.

The Mysterious Colonel Simon P. Kase

Not long after William Henry Chaney told his story, Col. Simon P. Kase became the first eyewitness to claim that Lincoln had definitely been present when the piano floated (an event J. C. Laurie either never saw or didn't mention). At the same time, Kase claimed that it was spiritual advice that convinced Lincoln to issue the Emancipation Proclamation.

Born in 1814, Simon P. Kase of Pennsylvania was a railroad developer, an inventor, a miller, and a foundryman; one biographical sketch describes him as "one of the most remarkable men of the day."[86] He may not have actually been a colonel at all, but he was certainly a committed spiritualist. When he died of old age in 1900, his will stated that if he won his outstanding lawsuits regarding the railroads he'd helped build, 75 percent of the money would go toward building a spiritualist temple.[87] Nothing came of it, as a judge dismissed the lawsuits in the end.[88]

Kase was in newspapers often during the latter part of his life; roughly half of the articles are about railroad matters, but the other half are about his dealings with spiritualism. Beginning in the late 1870s, Kase began telling a story of going to Washington on railroad business, meeting President Lincoln at the White House, then attending a seance where he saw a young medium channeling spirits who urged Lincoln to issue the Emancipation Proclamation. In many versions of the story, a piano-floating demonstration followed, sometimes with people, including the president himself, hopping on top of it to show that it could rise and fall no matter how much weight was put on top of it.

Nailing down a definitive version of Kase's Lincoln story is difficult because many versions were published between

1879 and 1891, and minor details changed every time. The earliest and longest version of the telling I could find was published in the Spiritualist paper *Mind and Matter* on April 5, 1879.

According to this version, Kase came to Washington at his nephew's request in July 1862 in order to lobby Congress to give him $450,000 in bonds toward building an addition to the railroad. Around the time he arrived, he wandered toward the house where he'd boarded in 1850 and saw the name J. B. Conklin[89] above the door. A disembodied voice at his side said "go see him; he is in the same room you used to occupy."

Conklin, according to Kase's 1879 version, was present and just sealing a letter when he arrived, and was somehow expecting him. When Kase entered, Conklin said, "Mr. Kase, I want you to carry this letter to the president."[90]

Kase tried to get out of taking the letter, but Conklin insisted, and the two of them headed to the White House together. Kase rang the bell, gave his name, and was told to go right in (apparently because the president had thought he was S. P. Chase, the secretary of the treasury). In some later versions, Kase wrote that Lincoln also seemed startled, or perhaps even frightened, by Kase's strong resemblance to George Washington (something Kase took pride in; in 1870 he claimed that spirits called him "materialized George").[91]

After some chatting about railroad matters, Kase gave Lincoln Conklin's letter, which asked for an interview with the president to speak on spiritual matters.

The president turned to Kase and said, "What do you know about Spiritualism?"

"I know but very little," Kase replied. "But what I know you are welcome to."

In later versions, this turned into Kase saying that he owed all he had to spirit guidance. In the 1879 story, Kase told him a long story of communications with his late mother, who told him all about the spiritual realm and brought him into the fold of the spiritualist religion (the details make up a large portion of the 1879 version, but are omitted from all others) Lincoln, according to Kase, agreed to see Conklin for an hour on the following Sunday, and Kase persuaded him to write Conklin a letter instead. Lincoln agreed, and Conklin disappears from the narrative at this point.

Kase then got to work on railroad matters. Some four weeks after meeting Lincoln, Kase claimed that a woman approached him in the street and gave him her card, saying "Call me when it suits you." Judge Wattles,[92] a friend who happened to be nearby, told him that the woman was Mrs. Laurie, and the spirits must have told her to give it to him, and urged him to go. "I have been twice to her house," said the Judge. "She lives in Georgetown and has a daughter, now married to a Mr. Miller. She plays a piano with her eyes closed, and the piano raises up and beats the time on the floor as perfectly as the time is kept upon the instrument, and they call it Spiritualism."

Kase said that he and Wattles went together to Mrs. Laurie's house that very night and were surprised to find both President and Mrs. Lincoln at the place, attending the evening's seance.

When things got underway, a young woman came walking toward the president in a trance, saying, "Sir, you have been called to your present position for a great purpose. The world is in bondage and must be set free. Liberty has been conceived, and is about to be born. A spiritual congress supervises the affairs of this nation as well as a Congress at Washington. This republic is the leading van of republics throughout the world."

For some half an hour, in Kase's account, the entranced young woman spoke to the president about the importance of emancipating the slaves, stating in no uncertain terms that the war could never end unless slavery was abolished.

When the young woman (whom Kase pinpointed in at least one 1879 article as Nettie Colburn Maynard)[93] awoke from her trance, she was much embarrassed and ran off.

It was at this point that Mrs. Laurie's grown daughter, Mrs. Belle Miller, sat down at a piano and began to play in a trance of her own, and the piano rose and fell in time to the music—at least four inches off the ground, even though Kase, Wattles, and two soldiers who had accompanied the president sat on top of it.

Kase actually didn't say anything about Lincoln riding the piano in his early accounts. In fact, he specifically described Lincoln as a spectator, saying, "(The piano's) motion was so violent that we got off it and stood alongside till she played out the tune. The President sat looking at us all through this performance, apparently much interested."[94]

Two nights after this seance, Kase returned to Mrs. Laurie's house, and again found the Lincolns in attendance, getting a similar lecture about slavery before the piano was played and levitated again.

This, according to Kase, was only a few weeks before the president issued his Emancipation Proclamation, the preliminary version of which was announced on September 22, 1862.

Naturally, historians who look carefully at the story have seldom taken Kase's yarn exactly seriously, though most who brush it off seem to be under the impression that the piano ride took place at the White House. At no point in this version of the story did Kase say that Lincoln actually rode on the piano himself or that any seance was held at the White House.

Minor details change from telling to telling, though; an 1882 version specifically describes Lincoln as simply watching as others rode the piano, but around June of 1888, Kase told an *Evening Sun* reporter that Lincoln did sit on it, and that "the piano jumped so violently and shook us up so roughly that we were thankful to get off it."[95]

Kase had spoken of piano-floating mediums before. In a letter to Samuel Watson in 1877, he told the story of a medium named M. R. Holien. "As to her gifts," he wrote, "they are numerous, and of the most sublime order. She plays the piano ... and frequently the piano raises up and beats the time perfectly with the music."[96] There was no mention that he had seen another medium do the same thing, with the President of the United States in attendance on top of the piano, though it certainly seems like the sort of thing he would have brought up. It was a year and a half later that he began telling his Lincoln story.

Given the changes in the telling, it seems likely that Kase was never being entirely honest with his tale. That he did go to Washington on railroad business is backed up by the Congressional Record, though the dates don't necessarily match his story: the "memorial" he presented to the Senate on behalf of the railroad is dated February 16, 1863. It may be that the matter wasn't really presented to the Senate until months after Kase did his work, or it may be that he was fudging the facts a bit in order to tell his Emancipation Proclamation story.[97]

In 1891, a few years after Kase's Lincoln story appeared in *The Sun*, the story was reprinted by the *New Orleans Times-Picayune*, whose reporter said "We looked up the above-mentioned gentleman (Kase) and had him go over his remarkable statements as printed in the *Sun* ... we confess to have become very much interested in the subject, and felt that while a certain amount of truth might attach itself to his statements, he was nevertheless the victim of some strange hallucination, and at most it was but a case of indescribable enthusiasm on his part—the result of mind and thought and intention bent upon the subject of spiritualism."[98]

Now, I'm skeptical of the *Times-Picayune*'s story of tracking Kase down; perhaps they were actually just re-running something from another paper, but I can't imagine a New Orleans reporter going clear to Philadelphia just to get an old man to retell a story about a flying piano, no matter who he said was riding on it. I think they had it just about right in their assessment of him, though; the impression I get of Kase is that he was an old man with sincerely good intentions who was willing to bend the truth a bit to support his cause (and perhaps his own desire take partial credit for the Emancipation Proclamation).

Kase turned into one of those "research rabbit holes" that I fall down now and then, where there are just enough biographical sketches and newspaper articles to put together a fascinating portrait of a very interesting man. But try as I might, I could not find a photograph of him, any data about when or how he became a colonel (assuming that he actually did), or any proof that he actually met Lincoln while he was in Washington to corroborate his own accounts of it. It should also be noted that the bill in the Senate introduced on his behalf to build the railroad failed to pass, a detail he always left out of the narratives. Most modern retellings seem to be under the impression that he was successful.

He does not seem to have been the kind of guy who would let facts get in the way of a good story, but, just as the *Times-Picayune* said, there may have been "a certain amount of truth" in his story.

R. D. Goodwin, M.D., responded to Kase's 1879 article with a letter to *Mind and Matter* stating that he'd been Conklin's roommate at the time, and met Kase. He further claimed to hold several letters from Lincoln and had personally urged him to sign the Emancipation Proclamation.[99]

Goodwin said he didn't remember seeing Nettie Colburn Maynard, the medium Kase said gave Lincoln the inspiration for the Emancipation Proclamation. And she denied that part of Kase's story in a letter to *Banner of Light*.

But she always said that Lincoln had been on the piano. It was she who provided the second eyewitness account.

Nettie's Tale

In 1891, Nettie Colburn Maynard, who had been bedridden with rheumatism for years by then, published a lengthy book entitled *Was Abraham Lincoln a Spiritualist?* In it, she told the story of her whole life, including her discovery that she was a medium with the ability to communicate with the dead, and her association with the Lincolns. According to her book, she gave several seances for Mrs. Lincoln, and at least a couple at which the president was present as well.

One of the seances she spoke of was almost exactly the same as the one described by S. P. Kase. Unlike most of

Kase's early versions, though, Nettie describes Lincoln as riding the piano himself as it floated up and down, and she places the date as some time later than he did.

Born in 1840, Nettie Colburn grew up in Connecticut, where, between bouts of sickness, she claimed to have experienced several instances of psychic phenomena, including observing her dying grandfather saying, "Millie has just been here" (referring to his wife, who had died years before). This, she noted in her book, was in 1845, a few years before Spiritualism became better known via the public demonstrations of the Fox sisters.[100]

Having discovered that she had inherited the powers of mediumship from the grandfather, she says in her book that she spent the late 1850s and the early days of the Civil War as a "spiritual lecturer." After the first major large-scale battle of the war, the Battle of Bull Run, a guest at one of her lectures asked how long the war would last, and a spirit replied through Nettie that it would "continue for four years." This was, Nettie pointed out, "a distinctly prophetic statement which after events fully verified."

Of course, in her book, she had the benefit of telling the story years after the fact, making it another in the long list of spiritual predictions that were claimed after Lincoln died and the war ended. Whether she actually made such a prediction in a lecture in 1861, before anyone knew how long the war would last, is anyone's guess until a contemporary account can be found, though Colburn did give the names of three living witnesses who could back her up at the time. None seem to have been contacted to verify the account, and the prediction doesn't seem to have made the press in 1861.

Of course, little of Nettie's activities from that era are that well known outside of what we have in her own book, and not all of the points can be confirmed. There are a few notices in papers from the late 1860s that refer to her as a spiritual lecturer, but we don't know much about what went on in her lectures at the time of the war at all.

In August of 1862, Nettie wrote, she found herself taken control of by a "congress of spirits," composed largely of famous politicians who told her it was important that she meet with President Lincoln as soon as possible. She ignored the suggestion at the time, having heard that spiritualists who tried to speak with the president were treated badly in Washington. Shortly thereafter, though, she received a letter from her brother saying that he was lying sick in a hospital and would die if he didn't come home to receive care. Nettie determined to go to Washington not to give Lincoln spiritual messages, but to get her brother a furlough. All the while, it seemed that every time she attended a "circle," the spirits would insist that she must speak to Mr. Lincoln.

While in the process of getting the needed furlough in Washington, she attended several seances at the home of Mr. and Mrs. Laurie in Georgetown. Here, she met Mrs. Laurie's daughter, Belle Miller, whom she described as "one of the most powerful physical mediums I ever met. While she played the piano, it would rise with apparent ease and keep perfect time, rising and falling with the music. By placing her hand on top of the piano, it would rise clear from the floor, though I have seen as many as five men seated on it at the time."

It was at the Laurie's house that Nettie says she was first introduced to Mary Lincoln, whom she described as looking "about thirty," though she would have been a decade older, and "lacking in the general control, demeanor, and suavity of manner which we naturally expect from one in high and exalted position." Mrs. Lincoln said that she had come to see the Laurie's daughter, Mrs. Miller, exhibit her phenomenal physical manifestations, and offered to make sure Nettie's brother got the furlough he needed.

Flush with relief, Nettie felt strong enough to perform another seance of her own that night, and for an hour fell under the control of spirits who used her to discuss politics with Mrs. Lincoln. She awoke from her trance to hear the First Lady saying, "This young lady must not leave Washington. I feel she must stay here, and Mr. Lincoln must hear what we have heard."

This, for the record, would have been a few months before Mrs. Lincoln spoke to Orville Browning about attending a seance at the Lauries'. Much of the believability of Nettie's account depends on whether that New Year's Eve seance she told Browning about was her first time at the house. Browning's account sort of makes it sound like it was, but it's not totally clear one way or the other.

In December 1862, according to Colburn's book, she was brought to the Red Parlor of the White House, where she was introduced to Mrs. Lincoln once again, and where Mrs. Miller, who had come along, seated herself at the piano and did her usual trick of making it rise and fall in time to the music while she played it. As she was finishing, the guests turned to see Mr. Lincoln in the doorway, having been attracted to the room by the sound of the piano.

Nettie and Mrs. Miller were presented to him at once.

"So this is our 'Little Nettie,' is it, that we have heard so much about?" the president asked, cheerfully. He engaged her in several questions about her mediumship in a kind and genial tone, and someone suggested that they form a "circle," right then and there.

In the middle of making such plans, Nettie wrote, she fell into a trance, losing all consciousness, and only heard from her friends afterwards that she had been speaking about the Emancipation Proclamation, which was days from going into effect. She did not say, however, that she gave him the idea for it. In fact, in May of 1891, she flatly denied that part of Kase's story in a letter to the *Banner of Light*, saying herself that she hadn't even met the president until December 1862, by which point the public had known about the coming proclamation for some time, the preliminary version having been published in papers in September.[101]

When she awakened from the trace, she wrote, she found Mr. Lincoln sitting in his chair, watching her intently. "My child," he said, "you possess a very singular gift, but that it is of God, I have no doubt. I thank you for coming here tonight. It is more important than perhaps any one present can understand. I must leave you all now, but I hope I shall see you again."

And so Nettie remained in Washington. Mrs. Lincoln allegedly got her a job sewing sacks of seeds for the war effort for a dollar a day, working from nine until three with an hour break for lunch. At night, she filled her time with circles and seances.

According to her account, the day when Lincoln rode on the piano at the Lauries' house was February 5, 1863.

The trip was said to be a spur-of-the-moment decision for Lincoln; he had apparently just left a cabinet meeting (presumably discussing the recently tendered offer from the French government to mediate in the war), and saw Mrs. Lincoln and friends getting into a carriage for Georgetown. "Hold on a moment," he said. "I will go with you."

At the Lauries' house, in Nettie's account, Mrs. Miller played several Scottish tunes for Mr. Lincoln on the piano, and then Nettie went under the control of a spirit named "Old Dr. Bamford" who was apparently a favorite of Lincoln's. Bamford gave the president some war advice, and predicted that Lincoln would be re-elected the next year when elections came around again (as of February 1863, this was far from a foregone conclusion; no one had been re-elected in a generation, and there was a general sense that the war wasn't going well, compounded by the controversial Emancipation Proclamation).

When Nettie came out of her trance, Mrs. Miller made the piano "waltz around the room." According to Nettie's version of events, Mrs. Miller played the piano (a three-corner grand), and it rose and fell in time with the music. Mr. Laurie suggested an additional "test," and Mr. Lincoln put his hand underneath it to see that it wasn't being lifted by "strength of pressure."

Nettie said that the president smiled and said "I think we can hold down that instrument," at which point he climbed up on it, joined by S. P. Kase, Daniel E. Somes, and a soldier (often identified as Major Daniel Sickles, though Nettie said she'd never met him until months later, at a White House seance), and the piano continued to wobble. One witness told Mr. Lincoln that when he told others what had happened, they would say, "You were psychologized, and as a matter of fact, you did not see what you in reality did see." The president allegedly quipped that "You should bring (each) such person here, and when the piano seems to rise, have him slip his foot under the leg, and be convinced by the weight of the evidence resting upon his understanding."

She then has Lincoln hopping down and saying, "was this not wonderful?" to Colonel Kase.

Colburn said she saw Lincoln a few more times during her stay in Washington, once going into a trance so a spirit could assure him (correctly) that rumored bad war news was not true. At one seance attended by Gen. Daniel E. Sickles, a "little Indian maiden" named Pinkie took "possession of my organism" and addressed an attending general by the Indian name of "Crooked Knife." On each occasion, she was assured that everything she said about the war effort while in her trance state was correct in all particulars by Mrs. Lincoln.

Her book goes on to mention a number of seances with the Lincolns by appointment in late February and early March of 1863, though generally there were no witnesses to them. Most are said to have taken place around one o'clock, when the president took his lunch break. Most of them would have taken place at the White House itself.

Shortly after the 1864 election, Nettie was called home, and Mr. Lincoln told her, "I am sorry you cannot remain to witness the inauguration, as you no doubt would wish."

"Indeed we would enjoy it," Nettie said, "but the crowd will be so great we will not be able to see you, Mr. Lincoln, even if we remain."

"You could not help it," he answered. "I shall be the tallest man there."

"What they predicted for you, Mr. Lincoln, has come to pass, and you are to be inaugurated a second time. But they also re-affirm that the shadow they have spoken of still hangs over you."

This "shadow," Colburn said, Lincoln fully dismissed, claiming that he was confident that "nobody wants to harm me."

This was the last time she would see him; the rest of her book details the rest of her life up until contracting the illness she predicted would be fatal.

In this prediction, at least, she was certainly correct. She died at her home in White Plains, New York, in 1892, a year after the book was published. A year before, the *New York Sun* had stated that several spirits, including Lincoln, had visited her in physical form.

Notes about what went on at Nettie's White House seances were apparently kept in great detail at the time, and the notes were placed in the hands of one S. B. Brittain, a publisher who planned to bring the book out in the 1880s. But these notes and the original version of the manuscript were all lost upon his death.[102] Nettie essentially wrote the second version of the book from her deathbed, claiming to get aid from Lincoln's spirit for help on certain names and dates that she didn't remember offhand.

Certainly, that Nettie did perform seances at the White House from time to time seems to be backed up by a number of sources. Professor A. B. Severance wrote to the *Banner of Light* to say that Mrs. Lincoln had come to him for a seance, in company with Tad, not long after her husband's death, and had told him all about having Nettie Colburn come to the White House.[103]

And there is actually strong contemporary documentary evidence that Nettie did meet Abraham Lincoln. Among the Abraham Lincoln papers at the Library of Congress is a letter of introduction for Nettie from Joshua F. Speed, a friend of Lincoln from Springfield:

Washington, 26 Oct 63

Hon A. Lincoln
Dear Sir

My very good Mrs. Crosby and Miss Nettie Colburn her friend desire an interview with you.

It will I am sure be some relief from the (illegible) of office seekers to see two such agreeable ladies.

They are both mediums * and believe in the spirits and I am quite sure very choice spirits themselves

Your friend,
J. F. Speed

* Mrs Cosby said she is not a medium[104]

The letter of introduction firmly establishing a true connection between Lincoln and Colburn, though its late date seems to contradict many of her stories. Courtesy Library of Congress.

This is a fantastic document, not only lending credence to some of Colburn's stories, but indicating that Lincoln and Speed must have talked about spiritualist matters before, and that Speed thought Lincoln would be interested to meet a medium.

Unfortunately, the letter also casts strong doubt on the bulk of Nettie's narrative. The October 26, 1863, date on the letter pretty well obliterates Nettie's claim to have given Lincoln seances in December 1862 or in February of 1863, the date she fixes for the piano-riding incident. That she would need a letter of introduction at all in October of that year pretty clearly shows that she couldn't have been on nearly as intimate terms with the president as of spring 1863, as she claimed in her book.

Indeed, many details in her book are impossible to verify. Though Nettie spoke of being a popular lecturer as of the time of the Battle of Bull Run in 1861, I couldn't find any mention of her as a lecturer in the papers from before the end of the war, even in the *Banner of Light*, the spiritualist paper from Boston. Her name starts appearing in those papers only in 1866.

I could only find one contemporary account by an outside party of one of Nettie's demonstrations at all, and it wasn't a flattering one. In 1866, a reporter attending a spiritualist meeting in Providence described her going into her trance state: "Nettie thereupon went off in paroxysms of jerks, twitches, and sundry other spasmodic operations involving some muscular effort, and supposed to be super-induced by the influencing spirits. To the unbelievers present, the exhibition much resembled that of a nervous female frightened by 'spooks.'" [105]

Once in her trance, "She did not announce the names of the spirits she represented; but, in an exceedingly artificial manner, commenced, with her eyes closed, the delivery of an address from 'we' the spirits. The burden of her talk was a commonplace and somewhat ungrammatical exhortation to progress, 'Go on, continue, persevere, and otherwise advance with the good work.'" [106]

No mention was made at the time of her having given seances for the president.

As soon as Colburn's book was published in 1891, people who'd known the Lincolns began to weigh in on it. Two days after running a story about the book, the *Chicago Tribune* ran an article entitled "Abraham Lincoln Not a Spiritualist." It quoted a man identified as Major Bundy ("a conservative spiritualist") as stating that while Lincoln was not a spiritualist himself, exactly, the main of Mrs. Colburn Maynard's story was true, and Lincoln accepted many tenets of the spiritualist faith. This was probably John Bundy, a Chicagoan who edited the *Religio-Philosophical Journal*, a spiritualist paper that he took over when the founder, his father-in-law was murdered by a "disreputable phrenologist." [107]

"There can be no question but that Mr. Lincoln sat in seances," he said, "and repeatedly had mediums at the White

House. I know positively that through his investigations he became convinced of the continuity of life and of communication between the two worlds. He was an unusually cautious, discreet man, and while quite probable that he received advice from the spirit world, it is also certain that he never blindly followed it... it is a fact, as has been stated, that Lincoln held seances with Charles Colchester... and I am able to say confidently that he held a seance with Mrs. Nettie Colburn."[108] He went on to claim that while Abraham was not a "confirmed spiritualist," Mrs. Lincoln was.

The same article also quoted John G. Nicolay, Lincoln's private secretary, who insisted without hesitation that Lincoln was no spiritualist, and flatly denied Colburn's story.

"Of course," he said, "I have no doubt that Mr. Lincoln, like a great many other men, might have had some curiosity as to spiritualism, and he might have attended some of these seances solely out of curiosity. But he was the last man in the world to yield to any other judgement than that (which) he arrived at by his own mature deliberation. He was not superstitious, nor did he have any spiritualistic tendencies. I have attended spiritualistic seances, not because I believed in them, but because I was curious to see the proceedings. They were such manifest humbugs that I usually came away disgusted. If President Lincoln ever attended seances, as alleged, it was with this same feeling of curiosity. But I do not remember that curiosity ever impelled him to attend a seance. He had more important business on hand during

those days. In any event, I can say without the slightest quali-
fication that a seance never occurred at the White House."[109]

A few qualifiers are in order when we look at Nicolay's
quote, though. The way that Colburn described the first
seance, it was no formal affair—just a spontaneous trance
and piano display that Lincoln happened upon by chance.
Had it happened that way, there's a chance Nicolay might
not have known about it. Furthermore, Nicolay does seem
to be doing what many of Lincoln's associates were doing
to Lincoln at the time: projecting his own beliefs onto him.
One could say the same for Nettie and all of her witnesses.

Several witnesses did come forth to back Nettie up,
including Mrs. Daniel Somes, who said that she'd seen Nettie give seances at the White House, and that her story of the
piano ride was correct in all particulars.[110]

Mrs. Elvira Depuy, too, said in the introduction to Nettie's
book that she had seen Nettie giving a seance at the Lauries'
house, with Mrs. Lincoln and Mr. Newton in attendance—
this would presumably be the night that Mrs. Lincoln spoke
to Orville Browning about. She stops short of saying she personally saw the president at any seance, though.

However, by 1891, many of the principal witnesses who
could confirm anything were dead. The only real, eye-hand,
high-placed witness to be asked for comment was Gen. Daniel Sickles, who gave an interview to, of all places, a Pottsville,
Pennsylvania, newspaper called the *Miner's Journal*.

The Sickles Revelation

Gen. Daniel Sickles, who is described as a witness at several seances in the book, was one of the most famous men of his era, but before the war, he was most famous for killing his wife's lover, who happened to be the son of "Star Spangled Banner" author Francis Scott Key, across the street from the White House in the late 1850s. His highly publicized trial ended with him being acquitted on the grounds of temporary insanity, which, depending on who you ask, may have been the first time that sort of plea was ever successful. He later lost his leg at Gettysburg, and arranged to have the leg put on display at the Army Medical Museum (which still has it on display). He was one of the most famous men in the country by the time of his death in 1914, when his funeral, will, and burial at Arlington National Cemetery were covered extensively by papers all over the country.

For much of my work on this book, Sickles's own response to the book seemed like a wide gap in the story—no paper I could find mentioned any response from him at all, though several named him as a witness to seances. However, in combing through issues of the spiritualist *Banner of Light* from the weeks following the publication of Colburn Maynard's book, I did come across a mention of Sickles having given a very negative response to the *Miner's Journal*, the newspaper of Pottsville, Pennsylvania. The good people at the Schuylkill Historical Society had a microfilm copy of *Miner's Journal* and were able to locate the article for me.

The surviving scan of the article was faint, and in some points illegible, but it turned out to be a real doozy. Sickles commented on the affair at length, touching a bit on Lincoln's own views on spiritualism, his relationship with Mrs. Lincoln, the veracity of Nettie's account and a bit about the dancing piano. Crucially, though he strongly denied most of Nettie's stories, he did confirm that Abraham Lincoln attended seances at the White House, making him perhaps the only non-Spiritualist to reach across the aisle to confirm such reports.

"Mrs. Colburn Maynard is wrong," Sickles said, flatly.[111] "I was not present at the time she alleges, nor do I know anything of that particular occurrence. Mrs. Lincoln was a devoted believer in spiritualism, and it was to please his wife that Lincoln, in the kindness of his great heart, attended those gatherings. Mrs. Lincoln was devoted to her boy, who died in the White House, and his death was a great blow to her. I believe that event prayed (sic) upon her mind, naturally superstitious, to such an extent that she was lead to believe that she could receive messages from the dead child. To this end she visited mediums, and they made her believe she was in communication with him. After that, at her suggestion, mediums visited the White House."

Sickles went on to describe how he and Mr. Lincoln came to be involved:

I was particularly hostile to spiritualism, and for that reason Mrs. Lincoln wanted me to be present. I cannot say positively that President Lincoln entertained the same views that I did regarding the matter, but in tender consideration of his wife, whom he always called 'Mother,'" he did not ridicule her belief as openly or in such a gruff way as I did. Nevertheless, he made sport of it and chaffed Mrs. Lincoln about her belief.

I well remember one seance at the White House. It was held in the red room. I do not remember the mediums present, but, like as not, Miss Colburn was one of them. Mr. Lincoln was there, and I was there in uniform, brass buttons and all. One medium, a young woman, went into a trance, or what she claimed was a trance, and in a slow, methodical voice, recited messages to Mrs. Lincoln and the president. Lincoln sat in his chair, half doubled up, listening, and at frequent intervals Mrs. Lincoln would address her husband or me in a way to show her firm belief in the spiritual origin of the words the medium was uttering. After the messages had stopped coming, the medium, still in the trance, was blindfolded and was led around the room, identifying those present. Finally she stopped in front of me and made some remark about my being a soldier. "There," exclaimed Mrs. Lincoln to her husband. "Do you believe now?

You see she knows what he is. Are you convinced?"
"Pshaw" said Lincoln, with a smile. "That's nothing.
A girl takes to buttons as a duck takes to water."

This lines up reasonably well with the 1866 account of
Nettie's appearance while in a trance, though the same could
probably be said for many other mediums.

Sickles went on to describe Mrs. Lincoln's attempts to
persuade her husband that the information came from a
supernatural source, which led to the story of Lincoln and
the piano:

> Mrs. Lincoln began to defend the medium, saying
> that although she had never had the slightest
> instruction in music, she could sit down to a
> piano and play the most difficult music, and that
> while she was playing the piano would dance up
> and down to the music. At that statement, the
> president's (illegible lines) ... he got up from his
> chair and went over to the piano, a heavy affair,
> that stood in the room. I shall never forget Mr.
> Lincoln at the piano. He couldn't play a note
> understandingly, but he sat down as though he had
> (illegible) music for years. He shoved his long, bony,
> strong legs under the instrument, stretched out his
> arms, and produced a serious of utterly discordant
> sounds on the keys. At the same time, the piano
> began to jump up and down. We were amazed.

But the amazement was short-lived—the president was using his knees to make the piano "dance," and, after a moment of bouncing it around, he turned and spoke with "an expression of mingled fun, seriousness, and sadness," saying something that is not entirely legible on the surviving copy of the article, but appears to be, "See, mother, our piano can dance, too."

"That broke up the seance," Sickles said, "and Lincoln went upstairs. The statement that Lincoln placed … faith in spirit messages or (illegible) their advice is false. He was not that kind of man. Such things would no more move him than they would move a mountain."

This tantalizing clue to the piano story infuriated Hudson Tuttle, who wrote the response in the *Banner*. "The President," he wrote, "at that appalling hour (or the Civil War) might have played the buffoon; but surely the plain, unpretentious story of Mrs. Maynard is the more credible of the two."[112]

That Lincoln would have played the buffoon doesn't shock me nearly as much as it did Tuttle; after all, as we've seen, I'm perfectly willing to believe that while he was plotting ways to guide the nation through its darkest hour, he was also planning to defecate in Austin Gollaher's hat.

But perhaps Tuttle was right to doubt Sickles's credibility. Remember, this is the guy whose main claim to fame was killing a guy due to temporary insanity, not to mention a guy who was recently the subject of a book entitled *American Scoundrel*. Could Lincoln have possibly really made a piano appear to "bounce" using his knees? It wouldn't be an easy trick.

Also, Sickles may have had a bone to pick with the Spiritualists. His father, George Garrett Sickles, was a member of the Spiritualist religion himself, and in 1887, several newspapers reprinted a *New York Sun* article in which he claimed that every night, spirits only he could see, led by some famous musician of the past that he couldn't identify, would come into his room to serenade him. "Surprising?" he said. "Not to me. I have had such experiences so often that my only sentiment was one of gratitude and pleasure."[113]

When the old man, a millionaire, remarried in 1881, the *Times* of Troy, New York, wrote that Daniel and the rest of George's children were opposed to the union and didn't attend, since it brought the bride into the massive estate. "Dan has given him trouble enough," the paper said.[114] As of 1891, when he spoke to the *Miner's Journal*, Mrs. Sickles was still in charge of the property, and Daniel would eventually sue in 1895. One can certainly imagine that Sickles might have simply been eager to speak ill of spiritualists when the opportunity came up.

Still, what we have here is a very rare example of someone reaching across the aisle. When people talk about Lincoln attending seances, they tend to fall along party lines: Spiritualists always said that he did attend them, and everyone else said that he didn't. Sickles was no spiritualist and doesn't describe Lincoln as one of them, but does seem to confirm not only that seances were held at the White House, but that Lincoln was in attendance.

So, Was It True?

So the flying piano story is a weird little puzzle—a frustrating jumble of changing stories, conflicting data, unverifiable facts, and doubtful information, with just enough corresponding accounts and confirmed data to make the whole thing impossible to brush off altogether.

One tempting scenario to imagine is that Kase, perhaps having seen the "bouncing" incident that Sickles described, started telling his story to papers a decade or so later, and it gradually got wilder until he actually had Lincoln riding the piano. Nettie, in this version of events, may not have remembered them, exactly, but based her telling on what she'd heard from Kase (though she knew he was wrong on the date). It's easy to imagine that Sickles's story about Lincoln making a piano bounce is the "kernel of truth" behind the whole story, and that everything else is just a tall tale that grew from that kernel.

However, looked at from another angle, Sickles's version of events actually strengthens the tale a bit. In it, we do see that Mary Lincoln had been impressed by floating pianos, and was eager to have her husband see it for himself. The fact that he initially reacted by joking around and demonstrating how such a trick could be done might have only made her more determined to take the president to the Lauries' house to see what Belle Miller could do.

And if we simply assume that Kase lied about the date of the "piano seance," in order to give the spirits credit for the Emancipation Proclamation, he and Nettie's stories would agree in nearly all particulars; she never claimed that Kase wasn't there, only that the date in his story was wrong. The February 1863 date attached to Kase's railroad bill in the Senate gives further credence to the whole thing happening when Nettie said it did. The February 13, 1863, date on Kase's railroad case in the Congressional Record leans toward Nettie being closer on the date.

So, even though neither witness is exactly reliable here, we can't necessarily say that Lincoln's piano ride didn't happen. In fact, though the details get too jumbled to say anything with certainty, all of the conditions are right. We know from outside witnesses that Mary attended seances at the Lauries' house, that Abraham sometimes attended seances with her, and that floating pianos were the sort of thing Mary was known to see at seances.

And though Kase's story that spirits talked him into the Emancipation Proclamation is almost certainly bunk, it is absolutely inarguable that Lincoln had been given advice, reportedly from spirits, about the subject of Emancipation. As early as September 1861, Lincoln received a long letter from one J. S. Hastings that touched on the subject (in the form of spirit advice), one of the countless letters of war advice he got from mediums and their followers, including Kase's buddy, J. B. Conklin.

Lincoln hated long letters, and probably never read the one that Hastings sent.

Or any of the long letters warning him about assassins.

Five

Who's Dead in the White House: Lincoln's Dreams

*I*n addition to giving us one account of Lincoln's famous "mirror illusion," bodyguard Ward Lamon gives what is probably the only known first-hand account of Lincoln's other, best known prophetic vision, one in which he seemed to dream of his own imminent assassination in early 1865.

In November 1864, Lincoln became the first president in a generation to win a second term, defeating Democratic challenger Gen. George McClellan, formerly his top general, who had, according to some, spent the first couple of years of the war sitting on his butt doing nothing in order to make Lincoln look bad so that he could beat him in an election. The thirty-seven-year-old general's strategy failed; Lincoln ended up winning twenty-four out of twenty-seven states.

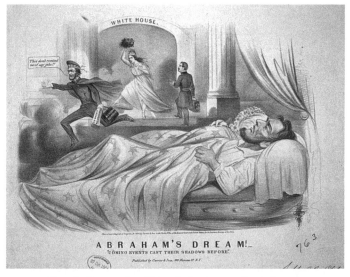

Years before stories of Lincoln having prophetic dreams circulated, an 1864 newspaper showed Lincoln predicting that he would be defeated by McClellan in the election. This particular dream did not come true. Courtesy Library of Congress.

The Democrats had run on a platform of negotiating a peace with the Confederacy, though whether or not to let them go on as a nation of their own was a divisive issue within the party. Only months before, it might have been an attractive platform to more voters who were growing tired of the seemingly endless, bloody, and costly war. By November of 1864, though, the war was winding down, and the Union was winning. The Confederates had reached their "high water mark," the farthest into the Union they were able to push, at the Battle of Gettysburg in 1863, which marked the end of Robert E. Lee's attempt to invade the North. Since then, General Grant had been pushing Lee's army farther and farther back, General Sherman was marching to the sea, and Atlanta had fallen.

By early 1865, it was only a matter of time before the war would end, and everyone knew it. Realizing that he had a window of opportunity to end slavery once and for all, Lincoln pushed the Thirteenth Amendment through the House of Representatives in January of that year and signed it on February first. Two days later, he met with representatives of the Confederacy to discuss possible peace terms, and let them know that accepting slavery's end was one of the two conditions he had for ceasing hostilities (the other being rejoining the Union).

However, he would not live to see it fully ratified by the states. Or to see the formal end of the war. The exact content of the peace talks are unknown, but Lincoln's terms were clearly unacceptable, as the South continued to fight to the last. And the assassination so many claimed to predict upon his initial election came to pass on April 14, 1865.

According to Ward Hill Lamon, only a few days before the assassination, on a day when Lincoln was in a "melancholy, meditative mood," he told Lamon, Mary, and perhaps a few others (the number of witnesses changes between tellings) about a strange dream he'd been having. Lamon claimed in 1887 that he took detailed notes on the events in the 1860s and was now trying to reproduce the story.[115]

Mrs. Lincoln, he said, was trying to cheer her husband up. He was roused a bit by her efforts, but then said, in low and measured tones, that "It seems strange how much there is in the Bible about dreams. There are, I think, some sixteen chapter(s) in the Old Testament, and four or five in the New, in which dreams are mentioned, and there are many other passages scattered through the book which refer to visions. If we believe the Bible we must accept the fact that in the old days God and His angels came to men in their sleep and made themselves known in dreams. Now-a-days dreams are regarded as very foolish, and are seldom told except by old women and by young men and maidens in love."

Here, Mrs. Lincoln interrupted to say "Why, you look dreadfully solemn; do you believe in dreams?"

To this, according to Lamon, Lincoln replied, "I can't say that I do. But one I had the other night has haunted me ever since. And since it occurred, the first time I opened the Bible, strange as it may appear, it was the twenty-eighth chapter of Genesis, which relates to the wonderful dream Jacob had. I turned to other passages and seemed to encounter a dream or vision wherever I looked. I kept turning the leaves of the old book, and everywhere my eye fell upon passages recording matters strangely in keeping with my own thoughts—supernatural visitations, dreams, visions, etc."

Lamon wrote that at this point (which couldn't have been any later than April 11, 1865, when Lamon was sent to Virginia, never to see his boss again), Lincoln seemed particularly grave, and Mrs. Lincoln said "You frighten me. What is the matter?"

"I am afraid," said Lincoln, "that I have done wrong to mention the subject at all, but somehow the thing has gotten possession of me, and like Banquo's ghost (in *Macbeth*), it will not down."

Mrs. Lincoln here expressed various assurances that she did not believe in dreams, but insisted that Lincoln tell the dream that had taken such a hold on him. After some hesitation, Lincoln gave in and told the story, reprinted here in full from the 1887 version of the story:

> About ten days ago, I retired very late. I had been up waiting for important dispatches from the front. I could not have been in bed long when I fell into a slumber, for I was weary. I soon began to dream. There seemed to be a death-like stillness about me. Then I heard subdued sobs, as if a number of people were weeping.
>
> I thought I left my bed and wandered down stairs. There the silence was broken by the same pitiful sobbing, but the mourners were invisible. I went from room to room. No living person was in sight, but the same mournful sounds of distress met me as I passed along. It was light in all the rooms; every object was familiar to me, but where were the people who were grieving as if their hearts would

break? I was puzzled and alarmed. What could be the meaning of all this? Determined to find the cause of a state of things so mysterious and so shocking, I kept on until I arrived at the "End Room," which I entered. There I met with a sickening surprise. Before me was a catafalque on which rested a corpse wrapped in funeral vestments. Around it was stationed soldiers who were acting as guards, and there was a throng of people, some gazing mournfully upon the corpse, whose face was covered; others were weeping pitifully.

"Who is dead in the White House?" I demanded of one of the soldiers.

"The president," was his answer. "He was killed by an assassin."

Then came a loud burst of grief from the crowd which awoke me from my dream. I slept no more that night, and although it was only a dream, I have been strangely annoyed by it ever since.[116]

Whether or not this really happened is (like everything else, as you've surely noticed) controversial among Lincoln scholars. Lamon does provide us with a first-hand, eyewitness account, but it wasn't published until twenty-two years had passed, when Lamon wrote it down for a newspaper (he had trouble getting high-profile jobs on his own merits, but by the 1880s he was much in demand from newspaper editors who liked his Lincoln stories). Even if Lamon really kept notes at the time from which he based the account, as he said he did, the actual notes apparently haven't survived, and none of the other people said to be present ever vouched for the tale, so it's tough to verify.

However, one thing that's almost never mentioned when the prophetic dream is discussed that this version, from 1887, is actually the second version of the story. Another, earlier, version appeared in the *Nashville Liberal* and was reprinted in several other papers (reprinted here from the *Daily Illinois State Journal*) in 1883.

The source of the story wasn't given in any paper I could find that reprinted the story in 1883, and I couldn't track down a copy of the *Liberal* itself (reprints of this story seem to be about all that survives of the paper at all), but the 1883 story is similar enough to Lamon's to make one suspect that the *Liberal* heard it from Lamon, though there are also enough significant differences to suggest otherwise.

The earlier version is worded differently enough that it's worth reprinting in full as well, for the sake of comparison (and because it's not very well known; the 1887 version has been reprinted countless times, but the earlier version doesn't appear to have been reprinted in over a century):

> It is not generally known that President Lincoln
> once feared he would be assassinated. While he
> was neither a professor of religion, nor even fixed

his belief in a particular creed, still he was fond of reading and discussing the Bible. On Sunday evening he invariably read a chapter or two from the scriptures, then gave his explanation of it.

One evening at the White House he read several passages both from the Old and the New Testaments relating to dreams, to which Mr. Lincoln and the children gave great attention. He began to chat with them on the subject of dreams and said he had been haunted for some days by a dream he had had. Of course, they all wanted him to tell it, though Mrs. Lincoln said she didn't believe in dreams at all, and was astonished at him. So he proceeded to tell it:

"About ten days ago I retired quite late. I had been up waiting for important dispatches from the front, and could not have been long in bed when I fell into slumber, for I was very weary. During my slumber I began to dream. I thought there was stillness about me, and I heard weeping. I thought I got up and wandered downstairs. The same stillness was there. As I went from room to room I heard moaning and weeping.

"At length I came to the end room, which I entered, and there before me was a magnificent dais on which was a corpse. Here there were sentries and a crowd of people.

I said to one of the soldiers: 'Who is dead
at the White House.'

He answered: 'The president.'

'How did he die?' I asked.

'By the hand of an assassin,' was the reply.

Then I heard a great wailing all over the house,
and it was so loud it seemed to awaken me. I woke
much depressed and slept no more than night.
Such was my dream." [117]

The story is the same in the main with a few minor differences, including the timeline: this couldn't have been as close
to the assassination as the 1887 version, since it refers to "the
children," and Robert wasn't at the White House in the weeks
leading up to the event (and wasn't a child, raising the possibility that it took place when Willie was still alive).

There are few ways to look at this:

Perhaps Lamon embellished the way he told the story
a bit over the years, perhaps expanding on it from earlier
notes for the longer 1887 version.

Perhaps W. S. Bailey, editor of the *Liberal*, heard it from
someone (Lamon?) and wrote it down himself some time
later based on recollections.

Perhaps Lamon just read the thing in the paper in 1883,
where it may have been told as pure fiction to fill space, and
then claimed it as a story of his own in 1887 (a year after W.
S. Bailey died and couldn't call him on it).

Or perhaps the unnamed source of the 1883 article was a second witness, lending the whole thing far more credibility.

The two versions also differ a bit in the way they end; the uncredited version from 1883 ends by stating:

> From that time until his death, Mr. Lincoln was haunted by the fear of assassination, and Mrs. Lincoln's first words after John Wilkes Booth had shot him on April 14 were: "His dream was prophetic." The remark was not understood then, but when the story of his dream was subsequently told it was explained.

Though Mary is sometimes quoted (perhaps erroneously) as having said "his dream was prophetic" at the deathbed, Lamon would not have heard it; he was in Richmond that night. Lamon's recollections include a handful of stories that he could only have heard second-hand, though, and the Mary quote appears in a collection of his reminisces of Lincoln collected by his daughter in 1911 (by which time Lamon had been dead nearly twenty years).

The 1887 version of the story, indisputably from Lamon, ends with Mary saying, "That is horrid! ... I wish you had not told it. I am glad I don't believe in dreams, or I should be in terror from this time forth." Lincoln responds with, "Well, it is only a dream, Mary. Let us say no more about it, and try to forget all about it."

It could also be worth noting that the *Liberal*, the tiny Nashville paper that published the story in 1883, was by no means a religious paper—in fact, when it's spoken of at all, it's generally thought of as a "free-thinkers" press, or even an "infidel paper,"[118] and the editor, W. S. Bailey, is generally spoken of as a born-again atheist;[119] about the only other thing I could find about it at all is that his daughter, who took over editorship upon Bailey's death, spoke of agitators who disapproved of her father's progressive attitudes on race and trying to destroy the press.[120] Few references to the *Liberal* survive, and possibly no actual issues of it at all. Though Lamon was doing a lot of newspaper articles about Lincoln in the 1880s, it's hard to imagine the tiny, independent *Liberal* as a good source for him, particularly for a non-political article with vaguely religious overtones. But it also doesn't seem like the sort of story that the nonreligious, Lincoln-supporting Bailey would simply make up himself.

In the 1911 collection of memories of Lincoln, Lamon (according to his daughter) said that Lincoln referred to the dream several times when speaking with him afterwards, closing one such conversation with a Hamlet quote: "To sleep; perchance to dream! Ay, there's the rub!"

Once, though, according to the 1911 collection, Lincoln made the dream into a joke while talking to Lamon. When Lamon expressed concern about the dream (as bodyguard, it was his job to be concerned for his boss's safety), Lincoln said, "Your apprehension of harm to me from some hidden enemy

is downright foolishness. For a long time you have been trying to keep somebody—the Lord knows who—from killing
me. Don't you see how it will turn out? In this dream it was
not me, but some other fellow, that was killed. It seems that
this ghostly assassin tried his hand on someone else. And this
reminds me of an old farmer in Illinois ... "

He then, according to the account, told one of his trademark folksy stories—this one was about a family using a
halfwitted boy to test greens that they feared were poison-
ous, figuring that "if he stands 'em, we're all right." "Just so
with me," said Lincoln. "As long as this imaginary assassin
continues to exercise himself on others, I can stand it."[121]

This brings up an interesting twist to the dream story—
could Lincoln have actually been having a prophetic dream
about one of the *other* assassinated presidents? The caskets
of McKinley and Kennedy were both in the East Room at
various times, both supported by the same catafalque that
held Lincoln's coffin. Although he specified the "end room"
in the dreams, Lincoln's own imagining of a White House
funeral probably would have placed it in the East Room,
where funerals were occasionally held.

Given that no source of the story exists from before 1883,
scholars are doubtful as to the tale's veracity. I lean toward
thinking it's true, but with some reservations. I'd love to think
the 1883 version was a second witness, but the part about "the
children" makes me think the dates in the two are so far off
that they must not both be actual accounts.

There's one other detail worth mentioning here: in 1883, Mary's quote about the dream being prophetic is said to clearly refer to the dream of the dead man in the White House. When it appears in the posthumous 1911 collection of Lamon's recollections, she's apparently not talking about this dream, she's talking about another dream.

The very morning of the assassination, Abraham Lincoln had spoken of another dream he'd had, one that he himself—without any question this time—claimed was prophetic.

Lincoln and his cabinet and General Grant; most of these men were present at the final meeting. From left to right: Stanton, Welles, Chase, Lincoln, Grant, Seward, Speed, Bates, Dennison. This was basically a version of Carpenter's First Reading of the Emancipation Proclamation *with Grant added in. Courtesy Library of Congress.*

I Drift ... I Drift ...

When Charles Dickens returned to England after his 1867–1868 American tour, he brought with him a story that Sen. Charles Sumner had told him at dinner in Washington, and that he now took to telling at dinner parties himself. George Eliot was particularly impressed.

In Dickens's version, on the morning of his assassination, Lincoln had gathered his cabinet together, plus a couple of major generals, and told them, gravely, that "something very extraordinary is going to happen, and ... very soon."

"Something good, I hope?" asked the attorney general.

"I don't know—I don't know. But it will happen, and very shortly, too."

The President then went on (Dickens probably used a special voice to impersonate him) to say that he knew something was coming because of a dream he'd had. He had had it three times before, all before battles such as Bull Run which were major losses for the Union. When asked the nature of the dream, he said, "Well, I was on a great, broad, rolling river—and I am in a boat—and I drift ... I drift ... "

Dickens was dramatizing things a bit, as was his wont. He used to particularly sell the pathos on the president saying "I drift ... I drift ... "

The story as Dickens told it was wrong on many particulars—either Dickens was exaggerating things or heard it wrong from Sumner in the first place (I suspect the former), but the main point of the story—that Lincoln had told his cabinet he knew something big was happening on the morning of his assassination because of a recurring dream of a sailing ship—is indisputably true. And here, for once, we have a paranormal story of Lincoln on which the sources are absolutely unimpeachable.

And, rather than only circulating years later, the story was well known within days of the assassination.

On April 18, 1865, just three days and four nights after Lincoln was shot, the *New York Herald* printed an account of Lincoln's last cabinet meeting. General Ulysses S. Grant, fresh from receiving Robert E. Lee's surrender, had arrived in Washington, DC, and attended the meeting, and he and the cabinet discussed their hope that soon General Johnston, too, would be surrendering to General Sherman, effectively ending the war. Unlike the Dickens version of the story, Lincoln, according to the paper, said he had reason to believe that good (or at least important) news was coming:

> "Well," said the president, "you will hear very soon now, and the news will be important."
>
> "Why do you think so?" asked the general,
>
> "Because," said Mr. Lincoln, "I had a dream last night, and ever since the war began, I have invariably had the same dream before any very important military event has occurred." He then instanced Bull Run, Antietam, Gettysburg, etc., and said that before each of those events he had had the same dream,

and, turning to Secretary (Gideon)Welles, said: "It is in your line, too, Mr. Welles. The dream is that I saw a ship sailing very rapidly, and I am sure that it portends some important national event." [122]

The story was printed in the *New York Herald*, which didn't give any real source as to who had leaked the tale to the press, but as the story spread to other papers across the nation, no one who had been present at the cabinet meeting denied that it had happened. Indeed, nearly everyone in the cabinet (and we're talking about some pretty high-level sources here) told their own version of the story over the years, and they differed only in minor points. Lincoln may have been only half serious, but he absolutely told the cabinet that he expected some important national event to come that day because of a dream he'd had of a ship sailing rapidly toward an undetermined shore.

Over the years, several people who were present told their versions to reporters or wrote down the tale in memoirs or diaries. This account comes from a diary entry by Gideon Welles, the secretary of the navy:

Inquiry had been made as to army news on the first meeting of the Cabinet, and especially if any information had been received from General Sherman. None of the members had heard anything… General Grant, who was present, said he was hourly expecting word.

The president remarked that it would, he had no doubt, come soon, and come favorable, for he had last night the usual dream which he had preceding nearly every great and important event of the war. Generally the news had been favorable which succeeded this dream, and the dream itself was always the same.

I inquired what this remarkable dream could be. He said it related to your (my) element, the water; that he seemed to be in some singular, indescribable vessel, and that he was moving with great rapidity toward an indefinite shore; that he had this dream preceding Sumter, Bull Run, Antietam, Gettysburg, Stone River, Vicksburg, Wilmington, etc. General Grant said Stone River was certainly no victory, and he knew of no great results which followed from it. The President said however that might be, his dream preceded that fight.

"I had," the president remarked, "this strange dream again last night, and we shall, judging from the past, have great news very soon. I think it must be from Sherman. My thoughts are in that direction, as are most of yours."

I write this conversation three days after it occurred, in consequence of what took place Friday night, and but for which the mention of this dream would probably have never been noted. Great events did, indeed, follow, for within a few hours the good and gentle, as well as truly great, man who narrated his dream closed forever his earthly career.[123]

Welles's account, as well as the early newspaper account, differs in two important details from the version Dickens heard: For one thing, in this version, the ship is sailing rapidly, not drifting slowly and dramatically. More importantly, in Welles's version, the dream usually came when good news was coming, and Lincoln, while expressing some belief that it meant good news was coming, believed that it meant that they'd soon have good news from General Sherman. But Welles himself added to it a little seven years later, when he wrote an article stating that Lincoln had said he and the ship were moving toward a "dark and indefinite shore,"[124] which seems like it would be an ill omen.

However, Dickens may not have been exaggerating too much. Attorney General James Speed was asked about the dream in 1885 by Joseph Hartwell Barrett, a biographer who'd heard the Dickens version, Speed confirmed that the dream had been told, but simply said "I cannot attempt to give (the story) in better words than Mr. Dickens."[125]

Another account is closer to what Dickens heard. Frederick Seward, assistant secretary of state under his father, William, was also present and wrote a version that's actually a bit closer to the Dickens version: he said that Lincoln had spoken of a peculiar recurring dream involving "a vague sense of floating—floating away on some vast and indistinct expanse, toward an unknown shore," and that "the dream itself was not so strange as the coincidence that each of the previous recurrences had been followed by some important event or disaster." To this, according to Seward, someone present suggested that perhaps when there was a time with possibility of great change or disaster, the vague feeling of uncertainty led to the "dim vision, and Lincoln thoughtfully said, "Perhaps. Perhaps that is the explanation." [126]

The mood at the cabinet meeting that day was light. In fact, Lincoln was in a better mood than usual. The war was going well, certain to end in victory soon, and his son Robert had returned from the army. It was not suggested at the time that the dream could relate to anything other than news regarding the end of the battle between General Sherman of the Union and General Johnston of the Confederacy.

Incidentally, such good news was coming. After the fall of Richmond and the surrender of Robert E. Lee days before, it didn't take a prophet to realize that the war was drawing to a close, and on the very day of April 14th, perhaps right as the cabinet was meeting, Confederate Gen. Joseph E. Johnston got word of Gen. Robert E. Lee's surrender to Grant, and sent a message to Sherman asking for a meeting to discuss the terms of his own army's surrender. At the meeting, Johnston would not only offer to surrender his own army, but to attempt to get President Jefferson Davis's authorization to surrender all remaining Confederate armies, ending the war completely without further bloodshed.

It would be a couple of weeks before all the terms could be agreed on, but just as Lincoln said his dream suggested, there was good news of huge national import coming.

A version of the tale also appears in Ward Hill Lamon's daughter's collection of his stories about Lincoln, though in his version, Lincoln was observing the ship, not sailing on it, and the ship was a Confederate vessel sailing away, with Union forces in close pursuit. He even added that Lincoln also saw, in the dream, the close of a battle on land, with "the enemy routed, and our forces in possession of vantage ground of incalculable importance."[127] Of course, Lamon was not in town that day and wouldn't have heard it first-hand.

In any case, the story very quickly became a part of national folklore—quickly enough that it became a part of Lincoln's own funeral. En route to his burial in Springfield, Lincoln's remains were essentially taken on tour, with massive funeral displays as the body lay in state in most of the major cities between Washington and Springfield. On April 23rd, it was brought to Philadelphia, where the coffin was laid in state in Independence Hall (the very place where Lincoln had spoken about the possibilities of being assassinated four years earlier). Among the countless wreaths and floral displays was one placed near the head of the coffin, bearing an inscription on a card:

"Before any great national event, I have always had the same dream. I had it the other night. It is of a ship sailing rapidly."[128]

Robert Lincoln, who had breakfast with his father that day, having just arrived with Grant following Lee's surrender, may have told the story as well in 1881. According to a legend often reprinted as fact, at the cabinet meeting that would turn out to be his last, President James Garfield asked Robert, now secretary of war, to tell the story of his father's dream. Some authors have given a dramatic account of Robert telling the dream of his father seeing himself assassinated.

These accounts are probably not accurate, though; I couldn't find any good account of Garfield's last meeting to begin with, and had Robert told of his father having a strange dream before being assassinated, it would have presumably been the story of the ship.

However, there may be some truth to the story: Right after Garfield was shot, days after the last meeting, the *New York Times* reported a conversation between Robert Lincoln and Postmaster-General Thomas James. "Do you remember," asked the postmaster, "how often General Garfield has referred to your father during the past few days?" "Yes," Mr. Lincoln replied, "and it was only the night before last that I entered into a detailed recital of the events on that awful night."

Whether this would have been at the last cabinet meeting is not specified; it seems like it would have been a solemn bit of entertainment at what was otherwise apparently a lighthearted meeting. Secretary of the Interior Samuel Kirkwood, who was present, said, "We had a long cabinet session, and the president was the life of the meeting. He interspersed the proceedings with anecdotes and jokes." No mention was made of any Lincoln talk at the meeting.

However, in the course of telling the story of Lincoln's last day to Garfield, it's entirely possible that Robert would have repeated the story of his father's dream of an indescribable ship sailing toward an undetermined shore.

In fact, Lincoln spoke about dreams often, and seems to have believed—or at least "half-believed"—in them off and on throughout his life. As with anything else to do with him, there's enough information either way that biographers can portray his belief in dreams—or lack of it—pretty well however they please, but here, at last, we do have some documentary evidence indicating that Lincoln was at least disquieted by dreams, enough so that he was led to take some action in his waking life based on them. In 1863, while Mary was in Philadelphia with their son Tad, Abraham sent her the following note:

Executive Mansion,
Washington, June 9, 1863,
Mrs. Lincoln,
Philadelphia, PA

Think you better put "Tad's" pistol away.
I had an ugly dream about him.

A. Lincoln.[129]

In 1863, when the letter was written, Lincoln was still recovering, psychologically, from the death of his son Willie, who had died the year before. Perhaps he was especially predisposed toward taking warnings from dreams seriously at the time. Still, this seems to show more of a "half belief" in the power of dreams than a hardcore belief that the dream of the pistol meant that something bad would happen; had he been truly convinced that the dream was an ill omen, he could have sent the army to protect them, not just a note.

So, though it's hard to say with any certainty that the "Who's dead in the White House" story is true, we do know that Lincoln was giving to telling people about his dreams, and that he was known to make fatalistic remarks about his own demise.

But such premonitions were certainly common as the war began to wind down.

Other Premonitions in 1865

It will be remembered from the introduction that *Macbeth* was a favorite of both Lincoln and his assassin. And that, according to the *Oxford English Dictionary*, it is the earliest known printed use of the word "assassination." And that Lincoln was reading lines about assassination in the play out loud only days before the event, almost as though he had a premonition.

Lots of minor things seem significant when considered in relation to the sudden death of the president. And in the days after the assassination, lots of small incidents earlier that spring seemed like grim omens.

Colonel William H. Crook, then a twenty-six-year-old bodyguard, also remembered a day just before the assassination, as he was walking with the president to the War Department, when Lincoln said, "Crook, do you know, I believe there are men who want to take my life? And I have no doubt they will do it."

"Why do you think so, Mr. President?" Crook asked.

"Other men have been assassinated," he replied. "I have perfect confidence in those who are around me—in every one of you men. I know no one could do it and escape alive. But if it is to be done, it is impossible to prevent it."

On the day of the assassination, he found Lincoln in a jovial mood, except that he didn't really want to go to the theater that night to see *Our American Cousin*. But he felt duty-bound. "It has been advertised that we will be there," he said, "and I cannot disappoint the people. Otherwise I would not go. I do not want to go."

This was surprising to Crook, who knew that the president loved going to the theater. According to Mr. Buckingham, the doorkeeper at Ford's Theatre, Lincoln would often slip into the theater unnoticed during a play and watch a few minutes of it from the back of the house before slipping back out and returning to work, just to "take a laugh." As Crook accompanied Lincoln back to the White House, Lincoln turned and said, "Good-bye, Crook."

"It startled me," Crook wrote, after years of time to reflect. "As far as I remember he had never said anything but 'Good-night, Crook,' before. Of course, it is possible that I may be mistaken. In looking back, every word he said has significance. But I remember distinctly the shock of surprise and the impression, at the time, that he had never said it before."[130]

Elizabeth Keckley, the Lincolns' dressmaker and tailor, came with a friend to what turned out to be Lincoln's final public speech on April 11th. As the crowd gathered around, she turned to her friend and whispered, "What an easy matter it would be to kill the president, as he stands there! He could be shot down from the crowd, and no one (would) be able to tell who fired the shot."[131]

Keckley related the thought to Mrs. Lincoln, who sighed and told her, "Yes, yes, Mr. Lincoln's life is always exposed. Ah, no one knows what it is to live in constant dread of some fearful tragedy. The president has been warned so often that I tremble for him on every public occasion. I have a presentiment that he will meet with a sudden and violent end. I pray to God to protect my beloved husband from the hands of an assassin."[132]

Rev. Thomas Bowman claimed that he had already been making grim warnings to Lincoln, based on nothing more than hunches. While serving as chaplain for the Senate in 1865, he was disturbed by the sight of an odd man prowling around the Capitol and the White House, and said that he warned Lincoln about him on April 9, 1865. The man he had seen was none other than John Wilkes Booth.

"The first time I recall seeing Booth," he said to a *New York World* reporter decades later, "was one morning just as I was about to open the Senate with prayer. The members were in their seats and stillness had come upon the gathering. I stepped forward and was about to speak when a man entered. He was so striking and handsome as to attract attention anywhere, but that was not what caused me to pause.

"The man made a peculiar impression upon me that I could not account for. He startled me, and I was so disconcerted that I could not go on ... it was a long time before I recovered from the shock of that man's appearance. I have never recovered from the impression I then gained, that he was there for no good and that his presence boded evil for some one." [133]

Booth was standing in the crowd at the same final speech that Keckley witnessed. As Lincoln spoke of making some of the newly freed slaves able to vote, perhaps right as Keckley was thinking of how easy it would be for someone to shoot him, Booth was urging one of his co-conspirators to do just that. Booth's response to the speech was to say, "That means nigger citizenship. Now, by God! I'll put him through. That is the last speech he will ever make. [134]

Booth himself would soon inspire ghost stories and urban legends that would become as much a part of our national folklore as Lincoln's own. On April 14th, hours after the cabinet meeting, Booth shot Lincoln in the back of the head as he sat in a box at Ford's Theatre, then fled on horseback. He was long out of town and on the run by the time Lincoln died the next morning.

Six

Booth and the Conspirators (And Their Ghosts)

On April 14th, 1975, the ninetieth anniversary of Lincoln's assassination at Ford's Theatre by actor John Wilkes Booth, actor Billy Dee Williams was onstage at Ford's, playing Martin Luther King, Jr., in a narrative tribute to Dr. King entitled *I Have a Dream*.

At one point in the first act, Williams (in character as Dr. King) was speaking of his reverence for the works of Abraham Lincoln and his role in the civil rights movement when something strange occurred: the sound of a person running across the stage, then out the back door—the very route Booth had taken. Everyone in the audience, from the front row to the back, was said to have heard it clearly, and the staff was puzzled. No one had been backstage at all.

It was later found that a live microphone had been dragged across the stage and out the back door, and the mic was later found in the alley. But who had dragged the mic?

John Wilkes Booth. Courtesy Library of Congress.

Frankie Hewitt, the executive director of the theater, flatly stated that "No one working at Ford's did that." [135]

Billy Dee Williams declined to comment on the ghost for this book (if I wanted to be really dramatic I could say "Mr. Williams was apparently so frightened that he refuses, to this day, to speak about the terrifying night ... "), but he's not the only person at Ford's ever to have an alleged encounter with the shade of either Booth or Lincoln. In the early 1980s, actor Hal Holbrook would, according to Hewitt, sometimes stumble in the middle of a speech, and explained to the director that "he felt a presence—a nameless 'something' coming from the Lincoln box."

People began regarding Ford's Theatre with superstition immediately upon its reopening to the public as a theater in the late 1960s (after years of other uses). Hewitt said that Presidents Johnson and Nixon had each declined four separate invitations to attend the theater at the last minute after previously accepting (though nothing odd happened when President Ford finally came on the anniversary of the assassination in 1974, just after taking office). Lincoln's ghost was reported more often than Booth's, generally appearing as a burst of sunlight in the box where he was shot. One actress in a gospel musical even walked offstage at intermission complaining that whoever was shining a light from the box was distracting her. (The box was closed to the public). [136]

Mysterious lights in the presidential box were commonly reported in the 1970s. Shortly before the playhouse was first reopened, there was a night during construction when all the lights in the box went out, though none of the lights in other parts of the theater did. They came back on, then went back off before coming back to life again. Workmen suspected a practical joke, but no one ever came forward to admit it.[137]

Paul Tucker, a speaker who gave lectures on the assassination in the theater in the 1970s, saw the ghost in the box one night. "I saw him sitting there," Tucker told a Florida newspaper in 1976. "He was in color. I saw about three quarters of his face. It struck me that what I saw was a little bit different than pictures I have seen—a human being."[138]

It may be worth noting that Lincoln's assassination is not the only tragedy that might have provided ghosts to the old theater. The government took control of the building immediately after the assassination, first leasing it and then eventually buying it outright. It was used mostly as offices throughout the late nineteenth century, though for some years it also housed the Army Medical Museum, where skeletal fragments of both Lincoln and Booth were on display (in an exhibit that pushed the bounds of good taste to the very limit). But the building fell into disrepair, and a collapse of the third floor in 1893 was one of the most gruesome tragedies in Washington, DC, history—more than twenty clerks were killed, and more than a hundred more were injured. But no one ever seems to have blamed the ghosts in the theater to that particular tragedy.

The boarding house across the street—the Peterson House—wasn't spared of ghosts, either. It was here that Lincoln died, having been carried across the street some time after being shot. Strange sounds have been reported there—one story went that a workman changing clothes in the house saw a ghost and was so scared that he ran outside in his underpants. Before tales of Lincoln haunting the White House became common, the Peterson House might have been his ghost's main stomping grounds; a widely printed newspaper article from 1894 stated that a man who recently bought the house was surprised when servant after servant quit after only a day or two on the job. "It is one of the traditions of Washington," the story said, "that the ghost of Mr. Lincoln returns four times a week to the house in which his spirit breathed its last the day after his shooting by Wilkes Booth in the theatre across the street."[139]

Joan Coleman, a tour guide at the house in the 1970s, was startled out of the place when she went to the third floor to raise the American flag one morning, having been startled by disembodied footsteps and the sound of jingling keys. "I asked if anyone was there," she said, "Then I heard the noise again. I ran as fast as I could across the street. It was a really frightening experience."[140]

The Assassin

The basic story of the assassination of Abraham Lincoln barely needs to be repeated: Having decided once and for all to kill Lincoln during his final public speech on April 11th, John Wilkes Booth crept into Ford's Theatre on the night of April 14th, where he'd performed often enough to have his mail sent there. Perhaps he was running lines from *Macbeth* in his head, "If it were done when 'tis done, then 'twere well it were done quickly. If the assassination could trammel up the consequence ..."

He snuck up behind the president and shot him in the back of the head before jumping to the stage and shouting "Sic semper tyrannis," breaking his leg in the process, before riding off on a horse he'd left with a stagehand outside.

On the run from the law after ten days (stopping to get treatment from Dr. Samuel Mudd along the way), he wound up hiding in a barn near Port Royal, Virginia, on the farm of a family who had not yet heard of the assassination. Expecting to be greeted as a hero throughout the nation, Booth learned after having dinner with the family at the farm that General Johnston had surrendered, which meant that his attempt to save the Confederacy by killing the president had failed, and made plans to flee to Mexico. Troops soon tracked him to the barn, setting it on fire in attempt to smoke him out. Though orders were to take him alive if possible, Sgt. Boston Corbett shot a bullet right through a crack in the barn, fatally wounding Booth.

This, anyway, is the established story. Exactly how much of it is exactly right is a whole other matter. What happened to Booth, both during and after the assassination, is a story shrouded in mystery, open questions, conflicting accounts, and, of course, more than one ghost story.

Accounts differ on what, if anything, John Wilkes Booth shouted as he jumped from Lincoln's box down to the stage. The most common, and generally accepted version, is that he shouted the motto of the state of Virginia, "sic semper tyrannis" (Latin for "thus always to tyrants"). Others who were present, though, said that what he shouted was "The South shall live," and others still said that he didn't say anything at all. "Sic Semper Tyrannis" is the most obvious candidate for what he really said; those who claim that he said nothing at all may simply not have heard it in the confusion, and if the phrase he shouted wasn't actually "sic semper tyrannis," it's hard to imagine how anyone would have gotten the impression that it was (Booth himself, in his diary, claimed to have shouted "sic semper," but not the last word).[141] Even with the general agreement that he probably did speak the Latin phrase, accounts differ as to whether he shouted it from the box before leaping to the stage or from the stage itself.

In any case, newspapers reported the next day that the phrase shouted was the Latin motto,[142] and at least ten witnesses spoke of having heard it from the stage within days of the event. The different accounts mostly came much later and can probably be chalked up to the general confusion that certainly reigned over the theater in the moments following the fatal shot.

Samuel J. Seymour, the last surviving witness of the assassination, was five years old at the time, and said in 1954 that after hearing the gunshot and watching Booth fall to the stage, his own concern was for the man who had fallen onto the stage. "Hurry, hurry, let's go help that poor man who fell down," he recalled saying in an article nearly ninety years later.[143]

For as thoroughly studied as the assassination has been, there's hardly one detail that isn't in dispute. Booth's drop to the stage was either a ten- or fifteen-foot fall, depending on the source, and because the theater was gutted in 1866, making exact measurements today would be difficult. Some say he broke his leg in the landing, others say he broke it later on. Some say he caught his spur on an American flag; others say he didn't. Some say an actress came and cradled the wounded president in her arms, and some say this story was bunk.[144]

Then, of course, there's the mystery of whether it was really Booth who was shot and killed in the barn at all.

The Mystery Mummy

It seems that nearly every time a notable outlaw is shot, word goes around that the death was a hoax. Practically every famous Wild West criminal who was gunned down is rumored to have escaped alive—Jesse James was even disinterred in the 1990s to see if it was really him in the coffin (it was). Booth is certainly no exception. Throughout the late nineteenth and early twentieth century, a number of men claimed to be the real John Wilkes Booth, perhaps most notably a man named David E. George, who died in 1903. George was the exact same age as Booth, had a leg that had been broken in the same place as Booth, and certainly seems to have believed, personally, that he was Booth. His body was embalmed and preserved so thoroughly that it could be, and often was, referred to as a mummy, and wound up as a carnival attraction for many years. (It was last seen in the late 1970s, and its current whereabouts are unknown—a mystery in itself.)

In 1907, one Finis Bates, David E. George's lawyer, published a book entitled *The Escape and Suicide of John Wilkes Booth* claiming that his client had, in fact, been Booth in disguise. He had met "Booth," who was then using the name John St. Helen, in 1877, and laid out his case in the book, showing photographs of George's corpse, dead at sixty-four in 1903 due to self-induced poisoning (and far more bloated than he'd later be as a mummy). He even included several pages of analysis of the lines and mounds on "Booth's" hands from Professor Bentley Sage, a palmist and clairvoyant who made a special trip to examine the dead man in the morgue, and said, "I discover this hand to be of the spatulate type, from which I learn that the subject was emotional, erratic, and governed almost entirely by inspiration."[145]

The body of David E. George, who is sometimes said to have been Booth in disguise, in the early twentieth century. Later photos of the "mummy" show a darker, more shriveled corpse. This one is said to have been taken eleven days after his death. Courtesy Library of Congress.

Bentley Sage appears almost nowhere else in history, though I did find a 1901 ad in the *Denver Post* in which Sage, "The Marvelous English Clairvoyant, Spirit Medium, Palmist" offered free readings[146] (and mining advice—his talents apparently included locating mineral lodes, which seems as though it could have made him a lot more money than fortune-telling), as well as several ads that he took out over the years advertising his readings from the parlors of various hotels. A 1905 ad lists several notable people whose palms he'd read (including Presidents Benjamin Harrison and William McKinley, Thomas Edison, murderer H. H. Holmes, and the King of Italy), ending with "David E. George ... who at the time of his death claimed to be John Wilkes Booth, and the photograph of his hand was taken and read eighteen months after his death,"[147] somewhat contradicting the story that it was done in the morgue. His ads were usually disguised as actual articles that happened to be buried among the ads for tooth powders and constipation cures that populated newspapers of the day.

That Bates gave such a witness so much space would do nothing to convince most skeptics, but the book did win a lot of support—even a 1923 note from the director of the FBI in Booth's file says "the work contains very strong evidence in support of the old belief that Booth did escape and live many years after the assassination of President Lincoln."[148]

The official story, that Booth was shot by Sgt. Boston Corbett in the barn at the Garrett's farm, is probably just about what actually happened, though the story contains several odd details that do nothing to quiet the suspicions. What's often left out of the story, and what may be the first reason that conspiracy theorists tend to think something was badly amiss, is that Boston Corbett was not exactly in his right mind.

Corbett had been a hatter for much of his adult life, and the phrase "mad as a hatter" doesn't come from nowhere—the chemicals hatters used in those days were known to mess with their minds. Whether his mental issues came from his trade is impossible to know, but Corbett certainly seemed to be mad by 1865. Lloyd Lewis, author of the 1929 text *Myths After Lincoln*, wrote that "Insanity had a peculiar focus upon Washington, DC, in that month of April 1865, and many a later historian would have gone mad among its tangles but for the occasional appearances among the yellowing pages of Corbett the Clown."

Born in England as Thomas P. Corbett in 1832, Corbett changed his name to Boston as a young man after being "saved" by a street preacher in that city. He began to wear his hair long and parted in the middle, a deliberate attempt to look more like the popular image of Jesus Christ. He spent the late 1850s traveling around as a street preacher himself, and, after joining the Twelfth New York Militia, became known among soldiers as the "Glory to God man" for his habit of praying constantly and loudly around the camps (his prayers were generally described as "whoops"). He was often in trouble for insubordination (for such offenses as telling the Colonel he was breaking God's law by swearing), and was once even sentenced to death for desertion after walking away from the unit, having been mistaken about the actual day on which his time was up (when he was pardoned, he reenlisted). He spent five months in the noto-rious Andersonville prison camp, then ended up with the regiment that surrounded John Wilkes Booth in the barn.

Corbett was under orders to take Booth alive, but when the barn began to burn in attempt to smoke him out, Cor-bett saw (or said he saw) Booth raising a pistol through a crack in the barn sheeting. Thinking that he had to fire in defense, Corbett fired a single bullet right through the crack in the sheeting and mortally wounded Booth. He later said that the wound he gave Booth was identical to the one Booth had given Lincoln, and that "God Almighty" had directed the shot.

It *was* a hell of a shot. An experienced marksman with laser attachments to help him aim couldn't have done it bet-ter. It's likely that the whole company could have spent all day trying to shoot a bullet clean through the crack, and not managed it. An officer said that God must have been direct-ing Corbett.

Of course, one should probably take into account that Corbett had also thought that he was acting under God's own direction on the night that he cut off his own testicles with a pair of scissors in a hotel room. Truly, to say that Cor-bett was a bit unbalanced is to greatly understate things.

Corbett never got the $75,000 reward for Booth's capture (which some cite as a clue that he didn't really shoot him). In the years after his brief turn as a national hero, he tried to make a living as a speaker, though his habit of turning every speech into religious whoops, rambles, and hollers made it hard for him to get any repeat business. He wound up working as a hatter again, then as a preacher, and then became a hermit. Convinced that Booth belonged to a secret society that had vowed to avenge his death, Corbett even bought a piece of remote property in Kansas on which to hide. Brought to court to answer charges of threatening to kill anyone who set foot on his property, he waved a revolver, pointed at his accusers, and said, "That's a lie, a lie, a lie . . . I'll shoot any man who says such things about me!"[149] It wasn't exactly the best way to defend himself against charges of threatening to shoot people, to say the least.

Boston Corbett. Courtesy Library of Congress.

In 1887, Corbett charged into the Kansas state capitol with a gun, announcing that he planned to kill the Speaker of the State House. For that adventure, he was sentenced to an asylum. After a year or so, he escaped and disappeared from the record; he's believed to have died in a major fire in Minnesota in 1894, but reports of him turning up in assorted small towns throughout the country, sometimes as a traveling medicine salesman, would be published in newspapers from time to time over the next several decades. There was even a rumor at one point that he'd been summoned from Mexico to determine whether the body of David George could have been Booth.

Hence, Corbett's strange life does nothing to quiet conspiracy theories.

Nor does the story that Booth was seen not long after the assassination at McVicker's Theatre in Chicago, where he had performed a few years before. It was probably just another actor who looked like him, unless, perhaps, Booth was really hiding out there while on the run. The theater was barely a block from the office of the copperhead *Chicago Times*.

Or, of course, one could always say that it was his ghost.

Booth and the Spiritualists

Less than a year after the assassination, a *Chicago Tribune* reporter attended a seance in a west side home in which the medium claimed to contact the spirit of John Wilkes Booth, a relatively rare instance of a spirit being called from Hell, a locale many Spiritualists denied existed.[150]

After a few preliminary festivities in which the half-dozen guests received messages from deceased friends, the spirit of Booth was called upon. He had apparently been called to the house several times before, and was always "very noisy and demonstrative." Never more so than this time, though.

Almost immediately upon making his spectral appearance, the ghost told the story of the night of the assassination, noting that he did not really break his leg in the fall from the stage, as was often said, but in a fall from his horse later on.

Here, perhaps, the spirit actually may have been exhibiting inside knowledge. Booth's own diary stated that he broke his leg while jumping to the stage, and this has been a widely repeated part of the story right through to the present day. However, despite the general agreement that the fall was hardly a graceful one, no witness to the assassination said that Booth seemed to have broken his leg until the twentieth century. Both David Herold, a co-conspirator in the assassination, and Dr. Mudd, who set the leg, testified that Booth had told them he had broken his leg in an accident with the horse.[151] Historians who examine contemporary accounts tend to agree that this is a more likely explanation than the tale that he broke it jumping from the box—that he could have escaped the theater, and the city, with a newly broken leg seems particularly unlikely.

The spirit communicated by pointing to letters and rapping on the table. Though Vice President Andrew Johnson had also been a target of assassination, the ghost said that he was now glad that Johnson hadn't been killed.

"Do you like Johnson?" the medium asked.

"Yes," replied the ghost, though he also noted that he didn't wish to see Johnson re-elected, preferring a McClellan/Lee ticket for 1868, as he believed that "they were the men destined to restore the powers of slavery and democracy."

"John," the medium asked, "are you in heaven?"

"No."

"Are you in the other place?"

"Yes."

"Is there a devil down there?

"Yes."

"Does he treat you rough?"

"Yes!" (the table rattled a great deal here).

"Do you think you deserve it?"

"No!"

One guest suggested that John should materialize or communicate in some more dignified way than simply rapping on a table, and the ghost replied that he would do so in a dark room, if the devil would permit it. The group (led by the table, which moved along) then went into a darkened parlor, but John never appeared. Knocks on the walls continued, though, and through them the spirit said he could communicate in writing. A medium, his eyes bandaged, let John write "through" him, and the paper was found to express the following:

"Johnson is trump. He went back on his party and is a Southern man at heart. Bully for him. He's a good democrat. Democracy will again be stronger than ever. Slavery will be established again ... McClellan and General Lee will be next President and Vice President ... Slavery and Democracy must flourish again."

He then said, "That reminds me of a story, as your Lincoln used to say ... " and used his time communicating from the great beyond to tell a rambling, painfully unfunny joke about an Irishman whose wife gives birth to a black baby. With the punchline delivered, he said, "I can't stay any longer; I'm wanted; see you another time; I must stand not upon the order of my going, but go at once."

With that, the spirit ceased communication, and after some tame encounters with less interesting spirits, the seance broke up, and the *Tribune* got the last word in: "It must be consoling to (President) Johnson to know that he has supporters and friends in another world, even if they are no more reputable characters than those who swear by him here."

In 1870, another Booth seance made the papers—buried at the bottom of the page in a Cleveland paper was a story of Booth being contacted at a Brooklyn seance, where he said he was sorry to have killed Lincoln, and that they had now been reconciled. The paper said that according to the ghost, "They are now good friends and walk out together." [152]

This was not the only time this type of story would go around; the idea that Booth and Lincoln were friends now seemed to please a lot of spiritualists. In 1905, a Brooklyn spiritualist told papers that Lincoln had told her that Booth's spirit had been weighed down by his awful sin, but when he entered the spirit world, he (Lincoln) was the first man he saw, and that the great man "held out his hand, and in that way became in effect the savior of Booth in the spirit world."[153]

The Ghostly Conspirators

Outside of his one-off appearance at Ford's Theatre while Billy Dee Williams was onstage, Booth's ghost has generally been quiet for the last century or so (or at least since spiritualism went out of vogue after its World War I–era revival). However, the plan that night was not only for Lincoln to be killed; another assassin who was involved in Booth's conspiracy very nearly succeeded in killing Secretary of State William Seward in his home. The man who was to kill Vice President Johnson apparently lost his nerve, though later eyewitness accounts state that Johnson was so drunk at the time that he would have been an easy target. Johnson was often said to be drunk more often than not; as a nineteenth-century vice president, he didn't exactly have many duties that required him to be sober.

In short order following the assassination, three surviving conspirators were rounded up, arrested, and sentenced to hang, along with Mary Surratt, the woman who kept the boarding house where they met. Samuel Mudd, the doctor who treated Booth for his broken leg, was sentenced to life in prison (though he was later pardoned).

Mudd's ghost was sometimes said to have made its presence known in his old house, particularly to his granddaughter, Louise Mudd Arehart, who credited his ghost for the inspiration to turn his home into a museum.

"I had heard footsteps going up the stairs," she told a reporter in 1983. "And knocks at my door. But every time I checked, no one was there. Then I saw Grandpa's ghost, and I saw him several times after that."[154]

But it's Mary Surratt who is most often said to have left a lingering spirit behind.

Mrs. Surratt

From the start, there has always been doubt as to whether Mrs. Surratt really deserved to be hanged. The Surratts were Confederate sympathizers, as were many in their native border state of Maryland, but whether Mary truly knew, or should have been held responsible for what was going on in her house was another matter.

John Surratt Jr., Mary's son, quit school to become a Confederate courier. John Sr., her husband, died in 1862, during the early days of the war, and two years later Mary moved to the family's city townhouse in Washington, DC, where she let out the upper floors to "gentlemen." Some have alleged that she moved to the city mainly to help her son's spy work, though there's no real proof.

John Wilkes Booth became a frequent visitor to the house; he had recruited John Jr. into a scheme to kidnap Lincoln in 1864, though nothing ever came of that one. After the assassination, authorities quickly identified Mrs. Surratt's house as a rendezvous point and meeting house used by the conspirators, and, though Mary was not directly involved, she lied to the officers, saying that her son had been in Canada. Searchers found pictures of prominent Confederates, such as Jefferson Davis, in her room, which was evidence enough of her guilt in those heady days. She was arrested and held at the annex to the Old Capitol Prison initially, then brought to the Washington Arsenal to be held in custody. Evidence against her was entirely circumstantial, but she was nonetheless convicted and sentenced to hang.

The federal government had never hanged a woman before, and more than half of the jurors signed a letter urging the judge to commute her sentence to life in prison (not necessarily because of innocence, but out of mercy, given her age and gender). Anna Surratt, Mary's daughter, tried in vain to get an audience with President Johnson to request clemency as her execution date approached, and was physically blocked by Secretary of War Edwin Stanton, along with Senators James Lane and Preston King. Johnson allegedly brushed off the requests on the grounds that Mrs. Surratt had kept "the nest that hatched the egg." Anna's pleas were so moving that many soldiers present were reportedly moved to tears, and she wound up spending much of the day sitting in the East Room.[155]

Even on the gallows, one of the conspirators is often reported to have said, "Mrs. Surratt is innocent. She doesn't deserve to die with the rest of us." (Although detailed accounts of the hanging don't mention him saying any such thing, according to the hangman, co-conspirator Lewis Payne made a similar remark in his cell the night before.[156]) Even hangman, Christian Rath and the guards expected last-minute clemency for her; Rath later claimed that he was told to build a gallows for four, but would probably only be hanging three.

However, all of the efforts, formal and informal, to save Mary Surratt were to no avail. She and the three men were hanged in front of a crowd of roughly a thousand, then buried in a shallow grave near the gallows. After being reinterred twice, her body was given over to her family in 1869, and she was buried at Mt. Olivet Cemetery in Washington, DC. Whether she deserved her fate remained a hot topic of debate for decades (and still is in some corners of the internet). Certainly one can imagine that if the murder of anyone else had been plotted in her home, her own execution would probably never have been considered at all.

As of 1971, it was said that occasionally Anna Surratt's ghost could still be heard banging at the door of the White House, hoping to secure an audience with President Johnson in order to beg for her mother's life in person.[157] Exactly where people got the idea that any phantom bangs that may occur on the door come from Anna is not really known, although some say that this only happens on the anniversary of the hanging,[158] which may provide a clue. In any case, it's hard to think of easy explanations for any mysterious knocks on that particular door—no one "doorbell ditches" the White House and gets away with it.

Judge Holt, the judge who sentenced Mary Surratt to die, grew a reputation as "the man with no heart," and he became a recluse. As early as the 1880s, his house was described as being overgrown with weeds and vines, and children were said to cross to the other side of the street when they had to pass it. He was seldom seen in public. After he died, the new owners of the house supposedly heard the sound of him pacing in the upstairs library. Years later, after the house was torn down, stories circulated that his ghost, clad in his army uniform, was sometimes seen walking down the road from his old house to the site of the old prison.[159]

His own supposed guilt was only the beginning of what some said was Mary Surratt's curse.

In 1878, the *Cleveland Plain Dealer* referred to "Martyred Mrs. Surratt" and said that her "murderers…died violent and miserable deaths." The report made an interesting case, particularly about the men who had stopped Anna Surratt from asking President Johnson for clemency—Edwin Stanton, and Senators Lane and King. Senator King killed himself in November 1865 by tying a bag of bullets around his neck and jumping from a ferryboat into New York Harbor. Senator Lane committed suicide the next year, shooting himself in the head while jumping from a carriage.[160] Secretary of War Edwin Stanton may not have been immune from the curse himself. He lived until 1869, when, four days after being appointed to the Supreme Court, he allegedly slashed his own wrists and throat with a barber's razor (though the story of his suicide was denied by the surgeon general himself, and modern historians tend to agree that he died of an asthmatic ailment). Suicide or not, dying so soon after his appointment qualifies as a tragic death.

Andrew Johnson himself, of course, who could have intervened in the hanging but didn't, was impeached by Congress and went down in history remembered better for his drunken antics and hostility toward freed slaves than anything else.

While her daughter bangs away on the door, Mary Surratt's own ghost is sometimes said to haunt the Old Brick Capitol building where she was first incarcerated, as well as the grounds where the Arsenal stood—one wonders if it ever appears on the gallows site today, now that a tennis court stands on the grounds. Some do claim that a boxwood tree that grew—apparently of its own accord—near the scaffold grounds was a sign of Mary keeping watch over the area.

Mary, indeed, seems to be nearly as restless a spirit as any other ghost connected to the life of Abraham Lincoln. In addition to the prison cells and grounds, there are numerous tales of her haunting her old house in Clinton, Maryland, and she's been blamed for strange goings-on at the site of the Washington boarding house. Annie Surratt had sold the place (at a great loss) after her mother's execution, and it changed hands rapidly enough to inspire stories that it was so haunted that no one could live there long.

Stories that the boarding house was haunted were published as early as December 1866, with reports that she was still wearing the robes in which she'd been arrested (it was widely reported that she was forced to wear the outfit she'd been arrested in all through her incarceration). The first new owner had vacated the premises within six weeks, "and was ready to swear with chattering teeth that his nervous system was shattered for a lifetime."

"Mrs. Surratt's house," wrote a Boston paper (quoted here from a reprint in the *Macon Telegraph*), "is haunted. There can be no reasonable doubt upon the subject. She herself persists in treading its halls, and perambulated these premises, in the dead of night, clad in those self-same robes of serge in which she suffered the penalty of the law. In costume, she differs from the 'woman in white' unmistakably, but that the general effect is none the less thrilling and altogether fatal to the composure of the observer, is positively averred by each successive occupant of the mansion." Children who lived nearby, it was said, stayed indoors at night rather than behold the old house after dark.[161] Like many ghost articles in old newspapers, it's hard to take the story too seriously, but the stories it told did become a part of local folklore. In later years, there were tales that one could still hear the whispers of the conspirators in the boarding house, or the footsteps of Mary pacing the second floor.

Reports appear to have quieted down after a century or so, though. Today, a Japanese restaurant operates successfully on the first floor.

Seven

Legends and the Ghosts of the Funeral and Tomb

A legend—which still pops up now and then—says that not only did a hush fall over the room in the Peterson boarding house the moment Lincoln died at twenty past the hour, but that the energy from the room affected the whole world to such an extent that to this day, everywhere you go, there is always a lull in conversation when the clock reaches twenty minutes past the hour.

It's easy enough to debunk this simply by checking your watch at a party, but it was a common superstition throughout the twentieth century; the urban legend fact-checking website snopes.com states that it comes from a 1948 book on superstitions—presumably Claudia De Lys's

8,414 Strange and Fascinating Superstitions. In that book, it was merely one example of common superstitions about lulls in conversations, and said to be believed by people who "believe the Great Emancipator died at 8:20 o'clock."[162] (For what it's worth, the time is a bit off.) In any case, simply for the legend to make it into a book at all seems to indicate that the superstition must have been well known by 1948.

A similar legend, which became very popular in the late nineteenth century, states that all display models of clocks and watches were set to a certain time (usually, though not always, said to be 8:18) because it was the time at which Lincoln died (or was shot, depending on who was telling the story). This time, we can at least trace the story back to something of a primary source. According to a widely circulated 1888 article (quoted here via an issue of the *Harrisburg Patriot*), an "observing man" had written a letter to the *New York Sun* asking, "Why it was that every clockmaker and watchmaker who slung an imitation clock or watch outside his shop as a sign had the hands painted on the face at exactly eighteen minutes past eight o'clock?"

*An illustration of Lincoln's ghost, haunting an early
incarnation of his tomb. Courtesy Library of Congress.*

Inquiries, it seems, were made, and various clock dealers
pointed investigators to W. L. Washburn, who made all of
the "dummy clocks" that were used as signs and advertisements around New York. He had been in business since 1853
and had pioneered the use of emblematic signs. By 1888, he
was apparently such an institution in the industry that any
sign maker in town who got a commission to make a clock
sign would send the business over to "Father Washburn."

A reporter dutifully called on Washburn, finding him a
happy old man with a long, white beard, busy at work painting
clock signs. Several clocks-in-progress were seen around the

studio, and, according to the reporter, "every blessed one of them had the hands pointed at 18 minutes after 8 o'clock."[163]

"When I painted the first emblematic (clock) sign," he said, "I don't know how I put the hands. All I remember about it is that it was for P. T. Barnum's old concern on Cortland Street, the Jerome Clock Company, since gone up the spout. I painted the hands any way I chose, up down, crosswise, or together, as my mood dictated, from that time up to April 14, 1865. That night the news was flashed into the city that Lincoln had been shot in Ford's theatre. I was working on a sign for Jeweler Adams, who used to keep a shop on Broadway, opposite Stewart's, at the time. I was making a great clock to hang outside (his store). Adams came running in while I was at work. He was a strong Lincoln man. He said, 'Point those hands at the hour Lincoln was shot, that the deed may never be forgotten.' I painted the hands, therefore, at eighteen minutes after eight. The idea struck me forcibly. I have never varied from the system since."[164]

Washburn also noted that having the hands at 8:18 was also good simply because it left room on the top of the clock for the shop's name, and he found that the Chicago and Cincinnati people were making display clocks the same way, though he doubted they knew the story behind the practice.[165]

The tale circulated very well in the late nineteenth and early twentieth century, and even inspired a brief movement after President McKinley was shot to have jewelers start displaying watches at the time of his assassination,[166] though nearly every mention of the tale in newspapers was accompanied by a gentle debunking of it (since dummy clocks weren't really displayed with the hands at the same time in every instance, and Lincoln wasn't shot at 8:18 to begin with). A quick check of clock ads in Victorian-era Sears Roebuck catalogs (which, incidentally, are the best bathroom reading in the world) show the hands displayed at seemingly random times.

Washburn, at least, was a real person. W. L. Washburn really did make watch and spectacle signs in a shop on Cortland Street in New York,[167] and a New York Comptroller's report shows that he'd been in business since at least 1863. Though I couldn't find any extant examples of his work to verify it, it's possible that he did get the impression that Lincoln had been shot at 8:18 and got into the habit of setting hands on the clock signs that he made to point at that time, and that dummy clocks at 8:18 were the norm in New York in the late nineteenth century.

But the practice was clearly never universal. The legend has evolved a bit over time; variations on it still circulate, but now the legend occasionally says that clocks are set at a certain time because it was when Walt Disney died.

Legends of the Funeral

Whether a clockmaker or two resolved never to paint clock hands another way or not, that wouldn't have been the oddest thing going on in the days after Lincoln died.

Lincoln's funeral was the most elaborate display of mourning the country had ever seen. The martyred president was embalmed (still a fairly novel practice at the time, though it soon became commonplace, partly because of a trend sparked by the funeral) and laid in state for public viewing in twelve major cities. All across the country, rural Americans lined up along the railroad tracks to pay their last respects as the Old Nashville, the Lincoln Funeral Train, rolled by.

The twelve cities, for their part, seemed as though they were trying to outdo each other for the most impressive setup. Black crepe was everywhere, mourners lined the streets, and thousands of citizens lined into city halls and state houses to pay their last respects to the earthly remains of Abraham Lincoln, his face now covered in chalk to mask the dark discoloration that resulted from repeated embalmings (prompting more than one smart-ass Confederate to remark that it was proof that he'd secretly been black all along).

Even in such an atmosphere, a few thought the funeral displays were over the top and in bad taste. In the background, cities were vying for the honor of becoming Lincoln's final resting place, which was still a subject of controversy during the funeral proceedings. Even as the coffin traveled across the nation, there was still some question as to where it was headed.

Springfield wanted the tomb to be in a prominent place (where local businesses could benefit from the influx of tourists) and had already spent a good deal of cash buying a prominent space downtown. Mary Lincoln, the grieving widow, was defiant, insisting that her husband had wanted a quiet, unassuming grave in an out-of-the-way churchyard. Only days before, in one of those moments that seemed eerie later on, Mary and Abraham had been riding a carriage in Virginia, touring places that had been vacated by the Confederates as the war wound down. When they stopped to wander through a country graveyard on the banks of the James River, Lincoln had said, "Mary, you are younger than I. You will survive me. When I am gone, lay my remains in some quiet place like this." [168, 169] If Springfield wouldn't put him in the quiet Oak Ridge Cemetery on the outskirts of town, she threatened to bury him in Chicago. There was also a rumor circulating that he would be buried in the crypt beneath the rotunda of the United States Capitol building, which had originally been planned to hold the remains of George Washington. [170, 171]

In any case, everywhere the funeral went, myths and legends and ghost stories followed in its wake.

Lincoln lying in state in New York. Secretary of War Edwin Stanton ordered all photos of the president's remains to be destroyed, but the photo from which this illustration was based was discovered by fourteen-year-old Ron Rietveld among the Nicolay-Hay Lincoln papers nearly a century later. Courtesy Library of Congress.

Perhaps the first legend of mysterious goings-on during the funeral relates to the first procession of the remains though Washington, DC. According to legend, as the casket passed by Ford's Theatre, one of the cornices fell off the building. It's now sometimes even claimed that the same thing happened when Kennedy's funeral passed the same theater, in those long lists of Lincoln-Kennedy coincidences that have been circulating since the 1960s (and are usually a mix of fact and fiction). Any damage to the theater during the funeral, though, was not noted at the time, and the main procession would have not come closer than a block and a half to Ford's Theatre in the first place. (The crowd may have backed up all the way up 10th street to the playhouse, though a picture of the theater drawn during the funeral doesn't indicate it.)

After lying in state overnight, the coffin was taken to a depot on New Jersey Avenue, again not passing by the theater as it took Abraham Lincoln out of Washington for the last time.

Albert Waud's drawing of Ford's Theatre (identified based on other contemporary drawings) during the funeral shows no sign of a procession passing, or even a crowd gathering. Oddly, the Library of Congress catalog description doesn't mention that this is Ford's. Courtesy Library of Congress.

Chicago, the last major stop en route to Springfield, made one major coup for its parade: attending the procession was a regiment of Confederate soldiers, now re-clad in Union blue, having taken an oath of allegiance that freed them from a nearby prison camp. The solemnity of the occasion was so strong that one *Tribune* reporter claimed that the arrival of the funeral train at 12th Street and Michigan Avenue (which was, at the time, right on the lakeshore) stilled the waters of Lake Michigan by mystic force alone, writing a passage later frequently quoted as, "The waters of Lake Michigan, long ruffled by the storm, suddenly calmed from their angry roar into solemn silence as if they, too, felt that silence was an imperative necessity of the mournful occasion." [172]

It's often the case though, that quotes like this that appear in later books aren't 100 percent accurate, and that's the case here. The contemporary article I found was worded slightly differently, stating "The bosom of Lake Michigan was as unruffled as the temper of a girl in her early maidenhood, and reflected back the shadow of the fleeting clouds just as a glass reflects back the image of the object placed before it. She looked a little turbid and discomposed near shore, but away toward the line of the horizon, there was a streak of blue, prophetic of the happier time in store for us, when these sad and mournful days shall have passed away."[173]

One thing strikes me particularly reading the *Tribune* article about the funeral—it quotes the plaque on the coffin as giving Lincoln's death date as April 17th. This was two days off; he had died on the morning of the 15th. Probably just a typo.

Another story in Illinois held that after the funeral, the brown thrush bird was not heard singing in the state for a year. This particular story may not have been noted in print at the time (1865–66), but it was certainly part of Illinois folklore a few years later. It was first broken to the larger public by John Hay and John Nicolay, Lincoln's secretaries, in an article for *The Century Magazine* in 1889,[174] in which they said (with some skepticism) that they'd been told the story by farmers in Illinois. The story became widespread enough that it even inspired a poem in 1894, the last stanza of which went:

When martyred Lincoln died,
The brown thrush sang for not a year—
Sang not of hope and duty clear
In sorrow laid its song aside
When martyred Lincoln died[175]

If the story of the waters and the brown thrush were true, they were the only things in the city that were calmed by Lincoln's funeral; many believe that Chicago outdid other cities in flashy displays of grief. The actual lying in state of the president's remains at the courthouse, though, was a tasteful affair. The body was laid out under a rotunda, and on the second floor a choir of German-American veterans sang dirges.

Two small ghost stories may result from this particular stop in the funeral's 1,700-mile journey.

One is that the choir on the second floor was eventually incorporated as the Germania Maennerchor (Men's Choir), and they constructed their own building, Germania Place, near Lincoln Park in 1888. It's now a venue for weddings, banquets, and the like. Several people who've worked there have told me that they thought it was haunted, though few specific stories have yet been collected.

Other ghosts were later reported in the courthouse itself; which, only a few years before, had hosted a Union rally at which the song "Battle Cry of Freedom" was premiered. The courthouse was said to be haunted itself only a couple of years after the funeral, and the story was reported all over the country.

The Court House in Chicago during the funeral;
later said to be haunted. The stream of visitors is visible
leading to the door. Courtesy Library of Congress.

The ghost, according to *Frank Leslie's Illustrated News-paper*, had been heard shrieking and moaning in a manner that "plainly proves the original died in possession of a remarkable pair of lungs." Police were stationed at exits in attempt to prevent the ghost from leaving. Describing the shrieks (in a day before recorded sounds were possible), the reporter said "If the reader has ever seen a strong man dying and suffering the most terrible agony, the sounds uttered have only to be recalled to have *daguerreotyped* the expression given to the mysterious noises that pervade the lower portion of the Court-House." [176]

That the ghost may have had something to do with Lincoln's funeral having occurred there was not really brought up at the time—Lincoln made no such wails on his deathbed, having lost consciousness instantly after the gunshot, and certainly didn't do any wailing during the funeral. One spiritualist claimed to do some spirit-guided writing allowing the courthouse ghost to write through her, and her writing described the ghost as "The spirit king—about four feet high, has a large roman nose, broad features, heavy, long, white whiskers down on the breast, very heavy hair hanging down the back, peculiar curl in the mustache. I, King the Spirit, have done all the mischief in the jail … unless the doors are unlocked, and the prisoners are suffered to breath fresh air … the house will be demolished down to the foundation stone." [177]

If the writing was accurate, it could be said to be a prediction of the Great Chicago Fire, which would lay waste to the city a few years later, taking most buildings Lincoln would have known in Chicago with it. But the Court-House itself largely survived the fire, at least well enough to stay in use as a prison for a few years before being torn down and replaced. The Chicago City Hall stands on the grounds now.

Funeral Train Ghosts

Early in my career as a ghost tour guide, one of the my fellow guides told me the story of the ghost of Lincoln's funeral train pulling into Chicago, elaborating a bit to add that Lincoln himself could be seen dancing around the coffin, laughing, with his flesh dropping from his face.

It's a fantastic image, though it doesn't really hold up to research; the flesh wouldn't have been falling off of Lincoln's face. He was embalmed so many times that he was effectively mummified; he was still in good condition in 1901, and might well still be today. (Some believe that the lime in the cement might have eaten through the lead coffin and the remains by now, but the staff at the tomb told me they expected it was still in good condition).

But stories of the ghost of the funeral train—complete with undead passengers—are not uncommon. Indeed, there are tales of the ghostly funeral train told all over the route the train followed (and a few places it didn't). Occasionally, it's said to be driven by a skeleton conductor or to have a skeletal band playing music as it rolls through.

Several sources over the years have quoted an article from the *Albany Evening Times* speaking about the phantom train, though they never actually gave a date for the article, which made it tough to look up. However, thanks to modern technology and the ever-increasing number of papers being digitized, I was able to pinpoint the actual article as coming from the March 23, 1872, issue.

The article was entitled "Waiting for the Train: Interviews with the Night Watchman—Story of the Phantom Cars." The relevant portion, which comes after describing the more mundane work of the night watchmen, is so cool that it's worth quoting in full. Though excerpts have been quoted before, it's never been reprinted unedited:

There is a supernatural side to this kind of labor, which is as wild as its excitement to the superstitious is intense. Said the leader, "I believe in spirits and ghosts. I know such things exist, and if you will come up in April I will convince you."

He then told of the phantom train that every year comes up the road, with the body of Abraham Lincoln. Regularly in the month of April about midnight, the air on the track becomes very keen and cutting. On either side it is warm and still; every watchman when he feels this air steps off the track and sits down to watch.

Soon after, the pilot engine with long black streams, and a band with black instruments playing dirges, and grinning skeletons sitting all about, will pass up noiselessly, and the very air grows black. If it is moonlight, clouds always come over the moon, and the music seems to linger as if frozen with horror.

A few moments after the phantom train glides by. Flags and streamers hang about. The track ahead seems covered with a black carpet, and the wheels are draped with the same. The coffin of the murdered Lincoln is seen lying on the center of a car, and all about it, in the air, and on the train behind are vast numbers of blue coated men, some with coffins on their backs, others leaning upon them. It seems that all the vast armies of men who died during the war are escorting the phantom train of the president.

The wind, if blowing, dies away at once, and over all the air a solemn hush, almost stifling, prevails. If a train were passing, its noise would be drowned in this silence, and the phantom train would rise over it.

Clocks and watches always stop, and when looked at are found to be from five to eight minutes behind. Everywhere on the road about the 20th of April the time of watches and trains is found suddenly behind. This, said the leading watchman, was from the passage of the phantom train.

One informant had commenced with another story of the "death engine" which preceded every train to which an accident would happen, when the stationman called out "train coming!" and we reluctantly came away from this garrulous watchman, whose life-work, both physical and spiritual, seemed a perpetual romance.[178]

Perhaps the most incredible thing about this remarkable article is the early date: March of 1872. Considering that not quite seven years since the actual train passed by, for Lincoln and his ghost to be spoken of in such gruesome tones was nearly unheard of, especially in the North. Ghost stories about Lincoln would not start to circulate in earnest for decades.

With that in mind, it's difficult to know just how seriously to take the article. After all, a train with hundreds of thousands of ghost soldiers carrying their own coffins that was going by fast enough to be gone in five to eight minutes would have to be going far too fast for anyone to make out any of the details.

Of course, it should be noted that very little of the story is directly quoted from the watchmen. It's possible that the watchmen gave a much more vague story about sensing the train, or about the clocks stopping, and the reporter filled in the details (which would do any ghost story writer proud) himself.

Though the train is sometimes said to haunt several places along the track, there are very few other first-hand accounts in circulation. Indeed, no one ever tried to use a ghost sighting to clear up the enduring mystery of exactly what color the train car carrying the coffin was (it was variably described as red or brown, and only in 2013 did chemist Wayne Wesolowski determine that it was a dark maroon, using an original window frame, one of the only fragments that survived a 1911 fire that destroyed the car).

But perhaps, if the ghost train was real, it simply no longer appeared as vividly as it had when the ghost first started to appear by the time the color of the car was lost to history. That such an event as the Lincoln funeral could inspire such an outpouring of mental energy as to leave an imprint on the environment is at the heart of many of the less-supernatural explanations some have attempted to apply to ghostlore—sometimes it's called a "psychic imprint" or a "residual haunting"; not so much a "spirit" as an echo. Making the hypothetical conclusion that such a thing is possible, it's to be assumed, logically, that the strength of the imprint would diminish over time, perhaps first appearing as a fully visible train, then as a translucent one, then as a vague haze, or a noise, or an unseen force that seems to stop the clocks for five minutes, then as simply a general feeling of unease, and then, after several years, as nothing perceptible at all.

In any case, no one seems to have seen the phantom train in years.

Mythology at the Tomb

Abraham Lincoln's tomb in Springfield, Illinois, is an imposing place. It stands beneath a massive obelisk in Oak Ridge Cemetery, fronted by a huge bust of Lincoln himself. Inside, one walks through a lobby and around a rotunda into a crypt where Mary Lincoln and three of her children are interred behind a wall. Opposite the wall is the solemn burial room where Abraham Lincoln himself lies buried beneath several feet of solid concrete topped by a marble marker. Around the marker are various flags and the line Stanton uttered at the slain president's deathbed: "Now he belongs to the ages."

Being a tomb, it's a solemn place by nature, but in practice, solemn reverence does not seem to be the order of the day. Signs on the outside say "Silence" and "Respect," but they seem to go unnoticed. On the day I came, a bus full of retirees had come, and they busied themselves with loud chatter, pretending to pick the statues' noses, and shouting "Say cheese!" outside of the burial chamber. These were not rowdy teenagers, mind you. They were retirees acting like rowdy teenagers. It's sort of charming, if you think about it from a certain angle, and, in my experience, is something you see at presidential tombs quite a bit.

President Roosevelt addresses the crowd at the rebuilt tomb. Courtesy Library of Congress.

For many years, up until his death in 1949, Herbert Wells Fay was the custodian of the tomb in Springfield. He was moderately famous in his own right and owned one of the world's largest collections of Lincoln memorabilia, if not the largest. Despite complaints that it turned the tomb into a dime museum, much of his collection was displayed in the entryway to the tomb itself during his time there, and he cheerfully used a pointer to tell the stories behind the relics to the tomb visitors. In 1946, a reporter for a Springfield paper described a visit.

"When I entered this sanctum with him," he wrote, "Fay handed me an old tassel. 'This is from Mrs. Lincoln's coat. She wore it the night Lincoln was shot.' I noticed several spots on the tassel. 'Those are Lincoln's blood stains,' Fay said, softly."[179]

By this time, at the age of eighty-seven, Fay owned over a million Lincoln mementos, including fifty-eight signatures, ten original portraits, and the original signed statement of Boston Corbett describing his shooting of John Wilkes Booth. As a side collection, he made recordings of hundreds of people whose voices he thought should be preserved for posterity, so that what they sounded like would not be a mystery for future historians. Lincoln's own voice is something of a mystery; he died more than a decade before the phonograph was invented, so no one can say with certainty which actor has done the best job portraying his voice. He's often portrayed in films with a deep, booming, authoritative voice, but contemporary accounts say it was much higher, with several traces of his rural Kentucky roots.[180] Lacking a recording, or sufficient technology to see and hear directly into the past, it will remain an unsolvable mystery.

Fay had enough relics to make an exhibit two miles long, but there was one relic he never did manage to display: Lincoln himself. And it wasn't for lack of trying. While the tomb was being rebuilt and repaired in 1930, he told the *Daily Illinois State Journal* that he hoped that one day, Lincoln's remains would be displayed above ground in a glass sarcophagus, for everyone to see.

"I believe," he said, "that the time will come when the public sentiment will demand that the body of Mr. Lincoln be placed in a sarcophagus for public view. Persons who visit the tomb from all parts of the country openly express this opinion."[181]

The plan doesn't ever appear to have been seriously considered. Perhaps, having dedicated his life to studying a man whom he could never see, though he was only ten feet away, he was a bit envious of the handful of surviving men who had seen the corpse on the few occasions when the coffin was opened after the initial interment. Due to various concerns such as reconstruction and maintenance, as well as fears of grave robbing (see next section), the body of Abraham Lincoln was moved several times in the first few decades of its existence, and viewed more than once.

The first posthumous viewing of the remains was in December 1865, when the coffin was moved from a temporary vault into the new resting place that had been created. Leon P. Hopkins, a plumber's assistant, cut a small opening in the lead casket so that six of Lincoln's friends could look in and identify the body.

In 1871, when the casket was moved again, Hopkins and the same six again made sure that the body was still inside the new sarcophagus, near the newly interred body of Tad Lincoln, who had died in Chicago and had been placed in the tomb alongside Willie and Eddie, the two other Lincoln children who had died and been moved from previous interments. (Willie's coffin had been removed from the Washington vault and made the journey to Springfield on the famous funeral train with the remains of his father.)

In 1887, after years in which the coffin had been held in a stone sarcophagus above ground (in between times when it was hidden, or buried in a secret shallow grave), the Monument Association decided to bury the body properly. Again, when they had the coffin out for transport, plumbers cut a small hole into the coffin, and eighteen people who had known Lincoln in life filed past, positively identifying the remains. Hopkins was the last to see them before sealing the coffin back up, and thereafter made a name for himself as "the last man to see Lincoln's face."

But the monument came to be in need of repair a few years later, and in 1901, the body was moved one more time. This time, Robert Lincoln, the president's surviving son, was determined that this burial would be the final one. Some years before, railroad car manufacturer George Pullman had been buried in Graceland Cemetery in Chicago with a steel cage, railroad ties, and an awful lot of cement to protect him against vandals or grave robbers, and Robert wanted the same treatment for his father. A grave beneath ten feet of concrete was planned, and on September 26, 1901, the casket was opened once more before it was laid to rest, if only so that something could be said in response to conspiracy theorists who insisted that the coffin did not really contain Lincoln's remains.

Sitting in a classroom that day, thirteen-year-old Fleetwood Lindley received a note from his father via a teacher, telling him to come as fast as he could to Oak Ridge Cemetery, but to tell no one where he was going. (The opening was done in secret to keep the press away). His father had viewed the body in 1887 and described the skin as being "the color of an old saddle."

Now Hopkins once again created the hole in the lead casket, bringing forth "a pungent, frighteningly choking" smell, and the party moved forward to view the remains. They were still a dark color (by most accounts), but covered in white chalk. The headrest had fallen away, causing the head to fall back and slightly to the side, but the body was still generally in good condition, with his short black whiskers still visible (though his eyebrows were gone).

When Fleetwood Lindley told the story to a *LIFE* magazine reporter in 1963, just before his death, he remembered it clearly. "Yes," he said. "His face was chalky white. His clothes were mildewed. And I was allowed to hold one of the leather straps as we lowered the casket for the concrete to be poured. I was not scared at the time but I slept with Mr. Lincoln for the next six months."[182] The year before the *LIFE* interview, he told the *Chicago Tribune* that "He looked just like his pictures."[183]

Over the years, several of the witnesses from 1901 visited the tomb again (their visits were recorded, and often published in local papers, by Fay). Another witness, J. C. Thompson, once said that Lincoln looked like "a statue of himself," a sentiment that had been uttered enough times over the years to spark a rumor—one which seems to have driven Fay nuts—that the body of the president had mysteriously turned to stone.

"Lots of people keep asking, 'Isn't it true that Mr. Lincoln's body is petrified? We heard that it had been turned to stone.' This story has been going around for years," he said in the 1920s.

Lloyd Lewis, in his seminal 1929 book *Myths After Lincoln*, traced the legend of the body turning to stone to a *New York World* article from 1865 that described the embalming process (and, in the process, publicized the story that Lincoln had twice exhumed his son's body to look upon it once again):

No corpse in the world is better prepared … three
years ago, when little Willie died, Doctors Bryan
and Alexander, the embalmers, prepared the body so
handsomely that the president had it twice disinterred
to look upon it. The same men in the same way have
made perpetual this lineaments. There is no blood in
the body; it was drained by the jugular and sacredly
preserved … all that we see of Abraham Lincoln is a
mere shell in effigy, a sculpture.

Similar comparisons of Lincoln's remains to a statue were
made all over. Embalming was still something of a novelty to
the Victorians, and papers described the process in gruesome
detail in all the cities where the body lay in state, sparking the
belief that persisted well into the 1920s.

The other myth that drove Hays mad was one which held
that, despite the repeated checks into the coffin to verify the
presence of the remains, Lincoln was not really in the tomb.
Despite the times it had been identified, some continued to
hear that the actual remains were lost.

"There's never a day goes by," Fay told Lewis, "without
someone—and most days, a lot of people—asking if it isn't
true that Mr. Lincoln's body is missing. From every state in
the Union, people come suspecting that Mr. Lincoln's corpse
is gone—lost or stolen … for over fifty years people have been
asking if the tomb was empty … there are thousands who
don't believe he's here at all. I never let a person get away

without having heard the proof that Mr. Lincoln's body is there under the catacomb floor, buried ten feet down in solid concrete, and I show everybody the photograph of the eighteen Springfield people who identified the corpse when it was put into the steel and concrete where it is today, but the story keeps on coming back to the tomb and I can't see that it gets any less for all the work anybody can do to kill it."[184]

Perhaps this, not his own curiosity, was why Fay wanted the body in a glass coffin, where he could let the skeptical mourners see it for themselves. But if people were under the impression that the president's body wasn't where it was supposed to be, they could hardly be blamed. It had been moved a lot over the years, had been hidden secretly away at various times, and once came close to being stolen.

In November 1876, the time of the near-burglary, the coffin was kept above ground in a white, marble outer sarcophagus. Visitors to the tomb who passed by it got much closer to the actual remains than modern visitors can, and the remains were much more vulnerable. Anyone who could pick a lock could gain access to the crypt after dark, and the sarcophagus wasn't expertly sealed.

Grave robbing was exceptionally common at the time, but the market was primarily for fresh corpses that could be sold to medical schools. It would take a really, really corrupt school to buy a corpse that, by all accounts, would have been easily identifiable as Lincoln's (besides being pre-embalmed and of little use for dissection). However, the body of A. T.

Stewart, the "merchant prince of New York," had been sto-len in May of 1876 and held for ransom, a story that was much in the news at the time. One would think that around this time, the Lincoln tomb officials might have stepped up security in case anyone was getting any ideas.

As a matter of fact, people were. At that time, a small band of counterfeiters were operating in Chicago, headed by one Big Jim Kennally (one of several Chicago crooks and gamblers to be known as "Big Jim" over the years). The group would often meet at The Hub, a saloon on West Mad-ison Street, barely a block from the West Washington Street row house Mary Todd Lincoln had purchased in 1866. One night, over a few beers, they hatched a plot to steal Lincoln's body and hold it for ransom until they were given $200,000 in cash and a full pardon for one of their colleagues.

They might have pulled it off on their own, but felt the need to bring in a more experienced body snatcher to help with the dirty work, and hired a man named Lewis Swegles, who convinced them that he was the "boss body snatcher of Chicago." Unfortunately for the would-be crooks, Swegles actually worked for the authorities.

For some time, the robbers planned every detail of the heist (with Swegles reporting them all back to his superi-ors). Finally, they took the trip to Springfield and made the journey to Oak Ridge Cemetery under cover of night, where they filed their way through the lock (none of them knew how to pick them, though they surely could have found someone at The Hub who could) and approached the sarcophagus, easily removing the lid, which was sealed only with flimsy plaster of Paris, not cement.

But detectives tipped off by Swegles were lying in wait right outside the tomb, and the men only had the heavy coffin about halfway out of the sarcophagus before they heard a detective's gun misfire. They fled without the corpse and were swiftly captured. Officially, they hadn't actually done much of anything illegal. They were eventually convicted only of the attempted burglary of a $75 coffin.

But officials at the tomb were shaken, and for some years, the body was actually hidden underneath a pile of lumber nearby the sarcophagus on the tomb grounds. For years, mourners filed past an empty marble box. After this story leaked, people can hardly be blamed for doubting that the body was where the tomb officials said it was.

Even after Lloyd Lewis's 1929 book pretty well debunked the "missing corpse" story, the questions didn't stop. When a *Tribune* reporter visited in 1931, just after the monument had been rededicated by President Hoover, Fay, the custodian, was talking with the reporter when a woman took him by the arm and asked, "Are you sure the body is still there?" J. C. Thompson, one of the men who'd viewed the remains in 1901, was on hand that day to state that it was, and that "any inference that the casket has been stolen and never recovered, or that the one lowered into the grave does not hold the mortal remains of Abraham Lincoln, is now set to rest."[185]

It was said at the time that the legends seemed as durable as the monument itself, but they seem to have largely died out today. Mikle Siere, the longest-serving employee at the tomb as of 2013, told me that he seldom heard either the "statue" story or the "missing corpse" story today. He was more apt to hear amusing anecdotes about visitors, such as a boy asking whether Michael Jordan could afford a tomb like this one.

There are definitely legends, rumors, and misconceptions about the tomb that keep popping up, though—Siere specifically referenced stories that Mary Lincoln was not actually in her tomb, but buried with her husband beneath the cement. "Where that came from I have no idea," he said, "but we've heard that." Wayne Temple, a Lincoln scholar, was said to have started the story that Lincoln was below the ground with Mary, but no one at the tomb knew why he thought so. Still, it came up a lot for a while, along with odd rumors that Ann Rutledge, Lincoln's first serious girlfriend, was buried someplace nearby.

And that's not to say there are no outstanding myths or mysteries surrounding the tomb. One odd story Siere has heard is that in 1931 when the tomb was rehabbed, there were actually five coffins removed from the wall across from Abraham's own burial space (he was not moved at the time). It should have only been four (Mary, Tad, William, and Edward). Abraham Lincoln II, Lincoln's grandson, had been interred in the tomb following his death from blood poisoning in 1890, but had been removed in 1930 to be reinterred near his father, Robert (who had opted to be buried in Arlington National Cemetery instead of the family tomb).

Some detective work shows that the fifth coffin probably was an empty one that had once contained Abraham II. According to a contemporary Springfield paper, his body was buried in a lead casket enclosed by an outer casket of walnut, which had decayed by 1930, when he was moved. "The lead box," the paper wrote, "was lifted out of the crypt and deposited immediately into a new casket of statuary bronze … tinners were put to work sealing it into a cypress shipping box."[186] No mention was made of what was done with the original, decayed casket.

In late 1931, the same paper went into more lurid detail of how the body had been moved (along with the other four bodies, which were moved into temporary vaults during the tomb's repair). The team assembled to move the body in 1930 (which included Mr. Fay) entered the tomb after visiting hours, swiftly breaking the seals to open the crypts. The wood part of Lincoln II's coffin fell away as soon as they laid hands on it. The metal inner casket was extracted, cleaned, and transferred to the new bronze casket as quickly as possible. No effort was made to open it. Again, though, no mention of leaving the original casket behind was made, though it's probably what they did.[187]

The 1931 article does seem to debunk any story that Mary was buried down below the catacombs with her husband. Days after the grandson's body was moved, the same team returned to move the other four caskets to secret locations in the abbey at Oak Ridge until the repairs on the tomb were completed a year later. Most of the coffins were said to be of the old-fashioned, "shoulder flare" style, except for Mary's, which was a more modern casket. If hers felt empty, the team said nothing about it.

But, as the article stated, "All were sworn to the utmost secrecy, for reasons that the public will readily understand."

If Fay knew anything that the public didn't about the tomb, he took it to his own grave, which lies right in the shadow of the Lincoln tomb, not far from the grave of Fleetwood Lindley, the last person to see the president's face.

Eight

Contacting Lincoln

Around 1890, sixteen-year-old Erich Weiss attended several seances led by a tailor-turned-medium in Beloit, Wisconsin. One night, the spirit of Lincoln began to speak through the medium. "My interest mounted high," he later wrote, "for Lincoln was my hero of heroes. I had read and studied every Lincoln book that was available at the time. I knew every published detail of the Great Emancipator's life. And I was vaguely conscious that night of something about the utterances of the 'spirit' that did not ring quite true.

"So, at last, I asked: 'Mr. Lincoln, what was the first thing you did after your mother died?'"

The spirit replied that he had felt very bad, and went to his room, refusing to speak to anyone for days. But Weiss knew that Lincoln's first act after his father buried his mother was to find a clergyman to read burial service over the grave. He then began to realize that no matter how many spirits showed up at the medium's seance, there were never more than three different voices, and they were the same three voices every time.

When he asked the medium why this was, honestly expecting an explanation that would give him insight into the spirit world, the medium stared at the young magician for a moment, then laughed and said, "Well, you've caught me; but you've got to admit that I do more good than harm by consoling sorrowing people who long for a message from their loved ones!"

"But surely," Weiss wondered, "all mediums are not like you. There must be some genuine ones."

"None that I know of," the medium cheerfully replied. "They're tricksters—every one of them!"[188]

Erich Weiss later found fame under the name of Harry Houdini. This experience led to his own decades-long quest to expose fraudulent mediums, though he genuinely hoped all the while to find a real one some day.

Such Lincoln-themed seances were getting more and more common in those days (which is also right when Simon P. Kase and Nettie Colburn's stories were going public). Plenty of mediums claimed to be able to contact the fallen president throughout the late nineteenth century, and more than a small handful never, ever simply grinned and said, "You caught me" when they were challenged. Some, in fact, were far more convincing than the tailor, giving verifiable information and perhaps even making accurate predictions that would have been far harder to fake.

Years after being disappointed by a medium who claimed to put him in contact with Lincoln, Houdini made a deliberate hoax image of himself conferring with Lincoln's ghost to demonstrate how easy it was to fake such pictures. Courtesy Library of Congress.

Given the popularity of seances in 1865, it's probable that mediums were claiming to be giving messages from Lincoln before the funeral proceedings were even over: the earliest account of a Lincoln seance that seems to have been recorded took place in early June of 1865, when one of Lincoln's old comrades found himself at a circle and took the opportunity to inquire, through a veil of skepticism, whether Mr. Lincoln had anything to say. He was impressed with the results.

Carl Schurz, a Gettysburg veteran and former ambassador to Spain, was summoned to Washington in 1865 to speak with newly minted President Johnson. Along the way, on June 7,[189] he stopped to visit friends who happened to be planning a seance for that very night; they had been consulting mediums to receive messages from two sons who had been lost in the war, and a surviving teenage daughter was showing talent as a "writing medium."

"When the circle was formed around the table, hands touching," he wrote in his memoir, "a shiver seemed to pass over her, her fingers began to twitch, she grasped a pencil held out to her, and as if obeying an irresistible impulse, she wrote in a jerky way upon a piece of paper placed before her the 'messages' given her by the 'spirits.' The names of various deceased persons known to the family were announced, but they had nothing to say except that they 'lived in a higher sphere,' and were 'happy,' and were 'often with us,' etc."[190]

Schurz was given a chance to ask for any spirit he might wish to speak to, and asked if he could speak to the ghost of Schiller, a poet from his native Germany, and was astonished when the girl began to write a few of the poet's more obscure verses in the original German. The fifteen-year-old girl didn't seem bookish enough to have waded through such a thick, obscure volume as the one in which the lines were written.

Now more intrigued, Schurz decided to push the boundaries of good taste and asked if she could also contact Abraham Lincoln, who was not yet two months dead. There was a brief pause, then the young woman announced that Lincoln had arrived and was ready to write through her. Schurz asked the spirit he knew why President Johnson had summoned him (Schurz) to Washington, and the girl wrote: "He wants you to make an important journey for him ... he will tell you tomorrow." Asked if he should accept, the girl wrote "Yes, do not fail."[191] The spirit's writing then predicted that Schurz would one day become the senator from Missouri, which made Schurz laugh, as he had no intention of ever moving there.

The next day, President Johnson asked him to visit the southern states to see how conditions were there, so that he could advise him as to reconstruction plans; his account of conditions still being imposed on black southerners amounts to one of the country's first official human rights reports. Two years later, a business opportunity brought Schurz to St. Louis, and in 1869 he was named the senator, just as the spirit of Lincoln had predicted.

By all accounts, Schurz wasn't being entirely honest when he said he would never have dreamed about being sent on a journey or becoming a Missouri senator; he was surely guessing, or hoping, that Johnson was planning to send him south, having just days before suggested to Johnson that he send some "worthy person" there. And he may have been attempting to secure positions in Missouri at the time, as well. Biographers have generally been unimpressed with the story, especially seeing as how Schurz didn't write it down until years after the fact. Still, this may be the earliest reported seance to contact Lincoln and was perhaps the most convincing, having given accurate predictions and having been reported on by a source who knew Lincoln personally and was respected enough himself to have schools, streets, and parks named after him all across the nation.

Schurz didn't come away completely convinced that he had really spoken to the spirit of Lincoln, but wrote that "we must conclude that there are forces active in and upon the human mind the nature of which we do not know. Scientific research has given names to these forces—'spirit communication,' etc.—but as to the nature of these forces, leave us in the dark... what they really are we do not know. It is so with a force which some centuries ago might have been called witchcraft, but has now become our familiar servant, electricity. We can make it active. We can control its activity and put it to all sorts of practical uses, but what electricity is, we do not know."[192]

The "Message Department" in the *Banner of Light* would report messages from Lincoln occasionally, speaking through a medium in their circle room. In an early appearance in 1867, Lincoln's spirit said that he had investigated spiritualism in life, and met some nice mediums, but was never fully convinced of the truth of it (which does seem to be just about right). "I bore about the same relation to a belief in or acceptance of spiritualism that I bear at present toward the reconstruction of the government," he said. "I hope that certain causes will produce certain results, but I do not know." He did say that he was a Spiritualist now, though, and said "I am indebted to your medium for the reception of certain private warnings with regard to my assassination, purporting to have come from my son Willie—and I now know they did come from him." He had received one such warning from Willie, he said, only a week or so before the assassination. Echoing some of his dream and presentiment stories (most of which weren't yet publicly known in 1867), he said, "I had a strange feeling with regard to that little message. Although I tried to forget it, still it was ever present with me."[193] He left after extending kind thanks to the lady whose body he was using to speak, leaving readers with the feeling that Lincoln had been a class act all the way.

This really does seem like a fairly accurate way of describing what Lincoln's relationship toward spiritualism was in life. Though stories that he took it seriously remain unconvincing, he didn't publicly say anything against it, either, even when he was accused in the press of holding seances. His "malice toward none, charity toward all" philosophy applied to the spiritualists.

Not every seance contacting Lincoln was quite as convincing. Most of the others on record seem to have been patently the work of charlatans, which doesn't necessarily make them less interesting to read about today. Like biographers, one could get a good sense of the politics and philosophies of mediums by the way they portrayed Lincoln, even within a decade of his death. Usually Lincoln was portrayed as a heroic martyr, probably often with a booming voice, but now and then he would show another side. In 1875, a Rhode Island paper reported that Lincoln, calling himself "Uncle Abe," had taken possession of a medium at a Lake Pleasant spiritualist camp and used the medium to spew forth a stream of swear words and racial slurs that the paper called "simply disgusting."[194]

Dr. Henry T. Child was a medium who traveled on the lecture circuit telling stories of a spirit named Katie King. In his seances, King and other spirits would appear inside of a cabinet, usually silently and not bearing any particular message (even of the simple "we are with you still" variety), but providing a great spectacle for anyone who came to watch. In 1874, Child spoke in his lectures of contacting Abraham Lincoln in a seance in June of that year.

At the seance in question, Katie King had appeared visually in a white robe (in the lecture, Child commented that "I have never seen Katie wear the same dress on any two occasions. Her wardrobe must be extensive.") After a spirit named "Black Hawk" threw blankets in everyone's faces, Lincoln himself made a visual appearance. "He stood just within the cabinet, being twice seen distinctly as the door opened. He was clad in white from his head to his feet. He endeavored to speak, but did not succeed. It is one of the most difficult things for a spirit to materialize its vocal organs ... Mr. Lincoln made a friendly gesture to a colored man who stood near him, and then disappeared."[195]

According to another account of the seance, a member of the circle asked if it was really Lincoln, and the spirit nodded his head. When he appeared a third time, it was only indistinctly, but he was seen to be holding an American flag. The title of the article, "Spiritual Clap Trap," gives some indication of how the reporter took Child's stories. Popular though seances were, they were seldom taken seriously by the press.[196]

In 1888, a story circulated that a group of Chicago spiritualists known as The Church of Nature were planning to hold a convention of their own at the not-quite-finished Chicago Auditorium Theatre (which, despite not being ready to open, had just hosted 9,000 attendees of the Republican Convention, the old Wigwam having been destroyed years before). The organizer, a "Mr. Dean," said that delegates were expected from all but the southern states, and "What is more, we shall elect our nominee … (Harrison and Cleveland will have) not a ghost of a chance."

Dean said that one of the Church of Nature's directors, Mr. H. B. Philbrook, the party's presumptive nominee, had received a spirit communication from Sen. Stephen Douglas asking that they start a new party, since neither the Republicans or Democrats had kept a hold on the people. Douglas told him that "We spirits are with you. We are neither Republicans nor Democrats. We want a new party." He went on to say that "Lincoln is with us. Lincoln has been importuning Mr. Philbrook ever since last November to form a new party. We count on his powerful aid." Dean was quite insistent that nearly *every* dead politician was on he and Philbrook's side; he allowed, though, that the ghost of William Henry Harrison might be prevented from helping due to "family reasons"—his grandson, Benjamin Harrison, was the Republican nominee (and would go on to win).

The spirits would be involved by "controlling" the delegates. "A delegate from California may be Abraham Lincoln, a delegate from New York may be Stephen A. Douglas." The spirits, Dean said, had a regular organization of their own, in which, he believed, Lincoln and Douglas served under Moses, who would himself be quite active at the convention.[197]

Philbrook had already been in the news in Chicago with his theories that spirits exerted a lot of control over the world. While the theory that Francis Bacon was the true author of Shakespeare's plays was popular at the time, Philbrook maintained that they were actually written by Homer, who was controlling Shakespeare. He also said that Jesus had been a medium controlled by the Biblical Abraham, and, months before the new party was announced, he said that Lincoln had been controlled by Thomas Jefferson, and that "Mr. (Grover) Cleveland is not President of the United States. Stephen A. Douglas is president (by controlling Cleveland)."[198] Philbrook's followers were certainly impressed by him, and the article announcing plans for the convention was reprinted in papers throughout the country, but the convention itself attracted little notice, if it happened at all. It doesn't seem to have taken place, which is a shame—even if there wasn't a single real medium present, it would have been a hell of a spectacle.

Letters Philbrook and Dean wrote to leaders of other third parties outlining a platform of prohibition, women's suffrage, and labor rights, though the only reply I could find was a letter from Belva Lockwood of the Equal Rights Party suggesting that they simply join her party instead of trying to absorb it. Perhaps they took her up on it and canceled their own convention; Lockwood was the first woman to appear on official presidential ballots in 1884, and did so again in 1888. She received a few thousand votes, and is far better remembered than Philbrook today.[199]

Philbrook's ideas, though, didn't die out. The notion that prominent politicians were "controlled" by prominent spirits survived; in 1910 one of the "Chief Men" at the Ohio Convention of Spiritualists said that Lincoln was controlling Theodore Roosevelt, in the company of "some powerful Indian spirit" and perhaps Caesar or Napoleon.[200]

As the nineteenth century progressed, mediums branched into spirit photography, regular portraits of sitters purporting to feature spirits in the background. One of the most popular spirit photograph supporters of the 1890s, though nearly forgotten today, was Dr. Theodore Hansmann of Washington, DC, who is sometimes said to have been one of Lincoln's doctors in life. Hansmann amassed a whole collection of pictures of himself surrounded by spirits including General Grant, Queen Isabella, and even a native of Atlantis. Through automatic writing, he even collected spirit signatures, as well as entire paragraphs and letters to him claiming to be from Lincoln, one of which, published in an 1895 article, even alluded to Belle Miller, the piano-tilting medium, stating, "I shall never regret my early transition to the higher life … I knew about all these (spiritual) things in my mortal days. I had Belle Laurie at the White House many times during the stormy rebellion to seek advice, how to proceed, from the higher-realmed men, and I got it, sir."[201] The "spirit," though, stopped short of mentioning the piano, and the letter would be of more historical value if it had been collected *before* Nettie Colburn's book came out.

The muddy newspaper prints of Hansmann's photos, which are probably all that survive of them today, are pretty obvious fakes; they show him surrounded by the heads of famous people who tend to look exactly like known portraits of them. The image of General Grant, for instance, is clearly that same portrait from the fifty dollar bill. The *New York Herald* and other reporters were often impressed with his sincerity after meeting him (though a quick trip to the Smithsonian to compare his portraits to portraits on display quickly cleared up the mystery of how the photos were made), but his family thought he was out of his mind. The kinder papers said he was being duped by others.

That most mediums were frauds was well known, even among believers. Houdini always maintained that he was not a skeptic at all, and he and other prominent "debunkers" believed their work was not to disprove spiritualism in and of itself, but to separate the real ones from the fakes. Though spiritualism and seances had remained largely the same sort of experience (with spirit rapping, floating objects, and controlled mediums) in the first couple of decades after the days of the Fox sisters, around the time of Lincoln's death, there was a rush of spirits appearing in photographs. Such photos were easy to fake even then, but there are some spirit photographers whose works have never been completely explained, and who still have their supporters today.

And at least one seems to have counted Mary Todd Lincoln herself as a paying customer.

William Mumler

Exactly how involved Mary Todd got with spiritualists following her husband's death is hard to determine. In an 1869 letter to a friend, Mary Lincoln wrote that "I am not EITHER a spiritualist," which seems a strongly worded refutation, but she went on to say, "but (I) sincerely believe—our loved ones, who have only 'gone before,' are permitted to watch over those who were dearer to them than life."

There's strong evidence that, while not necessarily a member of the spiritualists' religion, per se, she did believe, or at least hope, that mediums could put her in contact with the spirit of her husband and her lost sons.

While the only solid, reliable, and contemporary source about her spiritual seekings during her time as First Lady comes from the 1863 diary entry by Senator Browning, the fact that she sought advice and comfort from spiritualists and mediums after her husband's death is somewhat better established with photographs and court testimonies. Like any other part of Lincoln lore, those photographs and court testimonies are subject to doubt and scrutiny, but almost no one disputes the main point that Mary was interested in receiving messages and comfort from beyond. The only question is whether it was something she did from time to time, or something she was obsessed with. Evidence points mainly to the former, though her surviving son, Robert, always said that it was the latter.

Perhaps the best known of the mediums Mrs. Lincoln called upon herself was William Mumler, a "spirit photographer" who made a living taking pictures of people in which their dead loved ones appeared behind them. The exact method he used to get his photos is still the subject of debate today, and he still has supporters who believe that his photos were genuine. Photographs that appear to show a spirit are not difficult to fake, but photographs that appear to show a very specific one, who may never have been photographed in life, and who Mumler had never seen and had no photos of himself, are another matter altogether.

In 1861, Mumler was working in a jeweler's shop in Boston and was acquainted with enough photographers to get an idea of how the process of taking pictures worked. During an "idle hour," he decided to try it himself, and, according to his memoir, a spirit form simply appeared next to him in the negative when the picture was developed.[202]

The camera operator told Mumler that he had simply taken the negative of an old glass that hadn't been cleaned. Mumler wrote that he accepted the explanation, but still got a kick out of showing off the photo as a novelty. But when he showed it to a spiritualist, jokingly saying "no one was present but me when this photo was taken," the man had Mumler sign that to the back. Mumler wrote: "This photograph was of myself, by myself, on Sunday, when there was not a living soul in the room beside me—'so to speak.' The form on my right I recognize as my cousin who passed away about twelve years since.—WH Mumler."[203]

Though Mumler wrote in his memoir that he thought of this as a harmless prank that the man might show off in New York, but that could never trouble him much back in far-off Boston, the spiritualists were dumbfounded by the photo; an article in the spiritualist magazine *Herald of Progress* stated that "the new manifestation of spirit power, if it be such, commands most earnest attention and inquiry. No single phenomenon could possibly awaken deeper interest than will follow this new revelation."[204]

This is the kind of thing ghost story tellers have to watch out for. As a ghost tour guide myself, when I'm telling a story I know isn't true, I try to make it obvious that the story is a joke. But several of the utter nonsense stories I've made up to pass the time in traffic jams have ended up being repeated as true. Some of them end up on television.

This was the same situation Mumler found himself in 1861. He was not a spiritualist himself, though he was interested in the spiritualists' ideas and probably not averse to the idea that spirits could be photographed, when he suddenly found that a spirit picture he'd made as a joke was being held up as genuine in articles that spread far beyond Boston. He quickly copped to the trick and explained that it was just a form of double exposure.

However, when he gave the more rational explanation, a "scientist from Cambridge (who was) thoroughly acquainted with photography" assured him that one could make a double exposure like that in daguerreotyping, but it couldn't be done by photographing on glass. The spirit, he said, *had* to be real. The scientist persuaded Mumler to take some more pictures that very minute with a camera set up upstairs, and he was (again, this is according to his own version of the story) astonished to get more spirit shots. Immediately, he got enough bookings for sittings to keep himself employed for three months.

Spirits continued to show up in Mumler's photos—completely, Mumler said, of their own accord, and one does have to admit that it's odd that he was able to get spirits that people recognized into shots so often. The spirits in the picture, according to Mumler, tended to be whoever the living sitter wanted to see, whether a late relative or a celebrity such as

Daniel Webster, even sitting in whatever position the sitter "mentally desired." Some may speculate from this statement that the psychic energies of the sitters, not actual spirits, created the images.

Others say that the spirits are simply vague enough that with some imagination, sitters could see the spirit as whoever they wanted.

Some naturally didn't believe Mumler at all, and some believed that he was actively taking advantage of the bereaved (though it's also generally agreed that he gave them a measure of comfort in the bargain, as was often said of fraudulent mediums). P. T. Barnum, the sideshow and circus kingpin, thought spirit photos were a joke, and wrote, "Can human credulity go further than to suppose that the departed still appear in the old clo' of their earthly wardrobe? The fact that the appearance of 'the shade' of a young lady in one of the fashionable cut Zouave jackets of the hour did not disturb the faith of the believers."[205] Though not calling Mumler out specifically at the time, he was quite confident that the process could be faked.

Mumler practiced his trade fairly quietly, moving to a New York studio but attracting little attention from the press after the initial flash of publicity in late 1862, until 1869, when he and his then-partner, W. H. Silver, were visited by an undercover investigator. They had been charging the massive (for the time) sum of ten dollars for photographs. Silver explained that "because the spirits did not like a throng and…to exclude the vulgar multitude, the price was set at so high a rate."[206] The investigator asked for a photograph of himself with his deceased father-in-law, and was told that they couldn't guarantee that particular spirit would show up, but paid two bucks as a deposit, and ended up with a picture of himself and a spirit he didn't recognize. He had the two arrested for fraud, and they were brought to court in a widely publicized trial.

No one in court professed to be certain as to just how Mumler was making his photographs, though witnesses testified that it wouldn't have been impossible to fake them. One witness, Abraham Bogardus, said, "I am familiar with the science of photography; the pictures shown could be taken by several processes; the spirit form on these pictures could be prepared on another plate and then transferred to the picture." Lawyers for Mr. Mumler were indignant, stating that just because the photos *could* be faked didn't mean that they were, and began reading forty of fifty Biblical passages that claimed that spirits had voices and forms (particularly citing a passage in which a donkey sees a ghost). "Is it then impossible," they asked, "in these days that the spirits should appear, bodily, for the purpose of photography?"[207, 208]

The trial was such a circus that even P. T. Barnum himself showed up to testify a belief that Mumler was a "humbug." He said that he had corresponded with Mumler a few years before, and that, at the time, the spirit photography thing was "played out" in Boston, so Mumler had sent him photos that he himself cheerfully labeled "humbugs" showing spirits of Henry Clay, Napoleon Bonaparte, and William "Colorado" Jewett, a self-styled diplomat who had tried to broker a peace between the Union and the Confederacy during the war.

"I went to Mr. Bogardus yesterday," said Barnum, "and asked him to take my photograph with a spirit on it; I could detect no fraud on his part, although I watched him closely; the spirit on my photograph was that of the departed Abraham Lincoln. I didn't feel any spiritual presence." (The Bogardus photograph, which is still in circulation, is often credited to Mumler himself.)

On the stand in his own defense, Mumler said he had never refused any investigator who wanted to examine his process, stating that "I positively assert that in the taking of the pictures on which these forms appear, I have never used any trick or device, or availed myself of any deception of fraud in producing them…in regard to Mr. P. T. Barnum, I would say that I can solemnly make oath that I never communicated with him verbally or in writing."[209] It's worth noting that "celebrity ghost" photos, such as the ones Barnum showed off, weren't something Mumler was known for at the time.

The prosecution couldn't produce any clear evidence that Mumler had actually defrauded anyone with his photographs, so the case was dismissed. Mumler went right back to work.

It's generally said that his career was ruined after the trial, but it was actually a couple of years afterwards, in 1872, that Mary Todd Lincoln came to see him, sitting for what may be the most famous spirit photograph of all time. The photo-graph Mumler took shows Mary sitting, stone-faced and with a mourning veil lifted. (Many accounts of her going to Mumler say that she was still dressed in mourning for Abraham at the time, but it was more likely for Thaddeus "Tad" Lincoln by then; he had died at the age of eighteen in 1871 in a Chicago hotel). Behind her on the right is a "spirit" that clearly resembles her late husband; better reproductions of the photo also show a fainter image of Tad standing behind her on the left.

Her sitting made the news at once. In late February of 1872 and on into March, several newspapers reported that Mrs. Lincoln had been consulting with spiritualists in Boston—"incognito and closely veiled." According to the reports, she visited "a well known lady medium on Washington Street," and that "the spirit of her lamented husband appeared, and by unmistakable manifestations revealed to all present the identity of Mrs. Lincoln, which she had attempted to keep secret."

The *Boston Herald* said that they could confirm the story—Mrs. Lincoln had come to Boston and taken lodging at the Parks House under the name of "Mrs. Linder," remained in town ten days, and visited the medium frequently.[210] A February issue of the same paper even ran an article claiming that she had been to see Mumler, including a letter from Mumler himself, describing the photo and claiming that Mrs. Lincoln had come to the studio wearing a veil and using an assumed name. Though printing techniques at the time kept the paper from actually publishing the photo, Mumler sent them a copy, of which they said, "the resemblance of the principal shadowy imagine upon the plate to the martyr president is certainly unmistakable. The other developed shadowy figure is less distinct, but that of a tall, handsome boy who might be Tad."[211]

Though such reports should be treated with a measure of skepticism, Mary Lincoln was alive to contradict Mumler's story and she never chose to do so, even after he published his memoir in 1875, which spoke about her at length. In fact, she never publicly claimed that Mumler's account was wrong in any particular.

The 1872 photo has never been the sort of thing that convinces skeptics—Tad looks cartoonish, Abraham's hands appear smaller than Mary's—but Mumler's story of how the picture came to be, told in more detail in his 1875 memoir, is fairly convincing.

According to his tale, Mrs. Lincoln was traveling under the name "Mrs. Lindall" and came in wearing a mourning veil, effectively hiding her identity.

"What do you charge for these pictures?" Mrs. "Lindall" asked. Having been told the fee (which was presumably still in the ten dollar range), she decided to sit for a picture of her own. Mumler invited her to sit down, then went to his dark room and prepared a plate. When he emerged, she was still wearing the veil.

"Do you intend to remove the veil?" he asked.

"When you are ready I will remove it," she said, apparently greatly concerned with her anonymity.

She lifted the veil just before the photo was taken, but apparently was not recognized. Mumler marked the negative as "Mrs. Lindall" and sent it to be developed.

The famous 1872 "Mumler" photo, with contrast enhanced somewhat to make the "Tad" image on the left more distinct that it is in most versions. Courtesy of the College of Psychic Studies, London.

Mary came back to the studio a few days later, only moments after the pictures came in, in a batch with several others.

Mumler was now working in company with his wife, a medium herself. He wrote in his account that when she gave Mary the photograph, Mrs. Mumler instantly became "entranced" by a spirit, making the meeting into a brief, informal sort of seance.

Mumler's account of what happened is worth repeating verbatim:

(Mrs. Mumler) found the one marked "Mrs. Lindall," which she handed to her, and then continued the conversation with her friend, who, by-the-way, being of an inquisitive turn of mind, asked Mrs. Lincoln (who was at this time examining her picture closely) if she recognized the likeness? Mrs. L replied, hesitatingly, "Yes."

My wife was almost instantly entranced (by a spirit), and, turning to Mrs. L, said, "Mother, if you cannot recognize father, show the picture to Robert, he will recognize it."

"Yes, yes, dear," Mrs. Lincoln said. "I do recognize it; but who is now speaking?" she asked.

The control replied, "Thaddeus!"

A long conversation ensued. Mr. Lincoln afterwards controlled (Mrs. Mumler) and talked with her—so the lady-friend informed me who had thus unexpectedly been a witness of this excellent test.

When my wife resumed her normal condition, she found Mrs. L weeping tears of joy that she had again found her loved ones, and apparently anxious to learn, if possible, how long before she could join them in their spirit home. But this information of course could not be given.

Mrs. Lincoln then related how she left Springfield for the sole purpose of visiting my studio, and having a picture taken as a test. For that express purpose she traveled incognito. When she arrived in Boston, she came directly to my house, before visiting a hotel, for fear that someone who knew her might see and recognize her, and thus defeat the object for which she had taken such a long journey.

The picture of Mr. Lincoln is an excellent one. He is seen standing behind her, with his hands resting on her shoulders, and looking down, with a pleasant smile.[212]

So there it is in Mumler's own words—whether or not readers have believed him tends to line up neatly with whether they believe in spirit photography in the first place. The photograph is remarkably similar to the one P. T. Barnum had taken of himself—Lincoln's "spirit" is in just about the same place. Some say that Mumler made a fortune selling copies of it, though surviving prints are actually quite rare—I could only find evidence of two original prints in existence today, and never found any advertisement Mumler made in order to sell copies.

In any case, it does seem likely that Mary found great joy from the picture and impromptu seance. So far as is known, she truly believed that Mumler's photograph showed her with the spirits of her husband and son. If she was really just waiting to die and join the spirits, though, she would have to wait for another long decade—and her troubles were far from over.

Spirits in Court

In 1875, Robert Lincoln decided his mother should be committed to an asylum. He filed a petition with the courts in Chicago stating that she was *non compos mentis* and incapable of managing her estate, and submitted a certificate from Dr. Isham, the family physician, stating that he believed Mrs. Lincoln was insane.

Mary was taken quite by surprise in her room at the Grand Pacific Hotel in Chicago and taken to the courthouse at Hubbard and Dearborn, where Robert was waiting, along with the judge, jury, and counsel.

Robert's motives are still debated (Mary always believed he was trying to get her money; he certainly intended to be named conservator of her estate), and there seems to be little doubt among historians that this was by no means a fair trial, even among those who think she really was insane. The proceedings were, in fact, something of a farce. The judge on the bench was a known opponent of Abraham Lincoln. The jury was mostly made up of Robert's friends. Many believe that all of the seventeen witnesses had been coached beforehand as to what they should say.

For her own part, Mary had been given no time at all to prepare a defense or summon witnesses. She was not given a chance to interview potential jurors. In their 1959 book *The Trial of Mary Todd Lincoln*, James A. Rhodes and Dean Jauchius wrote, "she was being railroaded in a courtroom pungent with a kangaroo odor and manned by a jury having about it the air of one impaneled to convict."[213]

If an interest in spiritualism were evidence of insanity, than much of the American middle class at the time could have been found insane. But Mary's spiritualist leanings certainly came up in the testimonies. According to newspaper accounts, "The evidence showed that for several years she had been a confirmed spiritualist, and she believed that her husband's spirit was constantly hovering about her and directing her."[214] Many even noted a story she'd told that Lincoln's ghost had told her she would die on September 6, 1874, and that she carefully, perhaps even eagerly, prepared herself.

People in the courthouse took little notice of her as she was brought in. This would not have been the same courthouse where her husband had lain in state; even the portion of that one that had survived the Great Chicago Fire in 1871 was now out of commission, and a new courthouse had been built at Dearborn and Hubbard. Papers didn't mention it, but it stood on the grounds where Stephen Douglas, her husband's rival (and one of her own former suitors), had been pelted with produce for speaking his support for the Kansas-Nebraska Act two decades before. But news of what was happening spread, and soon the room was packed to capacity with curious onlookers. Mary must have been mortified.

The *Chicago Tribune*, one of the few papers that had a reporter on the scene, elaborated further (though they pointed out that they were politely declining to describe the scene at the Grand Pacific Hotel when she was told that she was being tried for insanity). According to them, it was Dr. Willis Danforth who gave the most damning testimony for a ghostly point of view: he was the first of the witnesses called, and said that he had treated Mrs. Lincoln professionally in November 1873 for several weeks, with treatment focusing on "fever and nervous derangement of the head."[215]

Mrs. Lincoln had, he said, "Strange imaginings ... (she) thought that some one was at work at her head, and that an Indian was removing the bones from her face and pulling wires out of her eyes." In September 1874, while being treated for a "debility of the nervous system," she said that "some one was taking steel springs from her head, and would not let her rest; that she was going to die within a few days, and that she had been admonished to that effect by her husband."[216]

Danforth went on to claim that Mrs. Lincoln imagined that she heard raps on a table conveying the time of her death, and would sit and ask questions and repeat the supposed answer the table would give. In order to make a final test on the reliability of the answers she got from the table rapping, she had a system of "putting the question in a goblet found on the table. (If) the goblet was found to be cracked, she regarded (it) as a corroboration of the raps."

Though Mary's sister had previously claimed that Mary was fairly indifferent to spiritualism, Robert said otherwise, claiming that she'd given valuable silverware to a "clairvoyant" woman who was one of his neighbors, and said in a letter to Judge Davis, "She hardly thinks of anything else … her only companions are spiritualists."

This was probably an exaggeration, but the spiritualism alone wasn't the only thing brought up against her. Samuel M. Turner, the manager of her hotel, said that in April she had come into the office complaining of hearing strange noises in the rooms, which left her afraid to be alone. She even claimed to see a strange man appearing and disappearing in the room, though the female staff left to stay with her saw no one.

A housekeeper said that Mrs. Lincoln was disturbed by one of the windows in her room, a window which she "imagined … boded ill." Another employee said that Mrs. Lincoln complained that voices were speaking to her through the walls and floors.[217]

One by one, people from the hotel where she lived and various doctors who knew her came forth to tell stories of observing Mary saying she believed she'd been poisoned by former rebels, that her son Robert was dying, or of seeing her mixing up medicines in an attempt to poison herself. Others spoke of her reckless spending habits. None seemed to believe it was safe for Mary to be left to her own devices. A kangaroo court it may have been, but if even half of the stories seemed believable, no jury would have decided in Mary's favor.

If her husband's ghost had truly been communicating with her, it would seem that he'd done her no favors. Barely five hours after being informed that she was being tried for insanity, Mary was found insane and sentenced to be confined to an asylum. The next day, the *Tribune* said, she tried to commit suicide, going from drug store to drug store attempting to buy a deadly mixture of laudanum and camphor (one of them, knowing her condition, prepared a mixture that was really "liquid burnt sugar.")[218]

She was confined to a mental hospital in Batavia, Illinois, for around a year, then let out after a second hearing which lasted all of five minutes (during which she was represented by Mr. Swett, the same lawyer who had worked against her in the first trial). Col. S. P. Kase, the floating piano witness, eventually claimed that only days before the second hearing, he had written a letter to Robert Lincoln about his mother's spiritualism, and stated that "if he left her in the asylum he would be responsible for any harm that would happen to her."[219]

After her release, Mary traveled through Europe for a few years, then went to live with her sister in Springfield, where she died in 1882 at the age of sixty-three.

At that time, sightings of her husband's spirit were only beginning.

Nine

An Odd Assortment of Ghosts and Mysteries

*A*braham Lincoln's ghost is said to haunt any number of places; looking around online could give one the impression that he's haunting every place he ever went, and a few that he didn't. Most of these stories grow more from Halloween articles when reporters need to fill space, and many just began as offhand jokes. They seldom have actual first-hand accounts attached to them.

*The Lincoln Room at Fort Monroe, where Lincoln is
sometimes said to appear beside the fireplace, deep
in thought. Courtesy Library of Congress.*

Though the house in Springfield is often spoken of as being haunted, and at least one old newspaper article claimed that Lincoln wandered the streets of the town at night, I couldn't find a first-hand account of any ghosts there, unless one counts the "two faces in the mirror" story.

Ghost-hunting groups and TV shows occasionally request permission to hold investigations at the Lincoln Home, but the staff there doesn't seem to be troubled by ghosts. The only story that curator Susan Haake even knew of concerned a story that Mary was haunting her own bedroom, and that tourists passing through were occasionally known to see the chair in her room rocking all by itself (which, considering the sitter was invisible, could have been attributed either to her own ghost or to Abraham's own). However, that story was eventually fully debunked; after years of service, a security guard admitted to the staff upon her retirement that she had rigged up the rocking chair with some fishing line to make it rock![220]

Reports that the tomb was haunted have popped up in newspapers and books from time to time, but seldom, if ever, with any details—most mentions of ghosts in the tomb are little more than lines in larger articles about presidential ghosts or Civil War ghosts, and generally don't amount to any more than a casual, "Lincoln's ghost has been seen in his Springfield tomb, his home, and at other locations."

The staff at the tomb don't seem to be afraid of ghosts, either. When I asked Mikle Siere, the longest-serving employee on staff, if he'd ever heard anything about ghosts in the tomb, he took a deep breath, paused to consider it for a moment, and said, "Well, I don't know much about ghosts, but I would think that if he were haunting any place, he'd be haunting a place where he actually was when he was alive."

This does tend to be the case in ghostlore: one most commonly finds ghosts haunting the places where they died; some ghost hunters outright reject the notion that cemeteries and tombs can even be haunted, because almost no one actually dies in them, unless they were buried alive (which Lincoln certainly couldn't have been, having been embalmed and re-embalmed many times in the days between his death and his burial).

But no theory that seeks to explain ghosts covers every ghost sighting, and it does seem like most cemeteries and funeral homes acquire a ghost story or two over the years. Stories of ghosts haunting places where they used to live or hang out come up more frequently than is sometimes claimed, and Lincoln is certainly said to haunt a place or two where he probably never set foot.

In fact, the earliest article I could find reporting a Lincoln ghost sighting came from Mount Pleasant, Iowa, of all places.

According to an 1869 issue of a local paper, two young women saw the ghost of Abraham Lincoln while going for a walk in the dusky calm that followed a classic, crashing Midwestern thunderstorm one early summer evening. The paper set the scene vividly, saying, "Old Sol (the sun) had retired to rest, and pulled the cover up over his head, and nary shine did he make. We suppose that it was quieter than twenty-seven graveyards—it always is upon such occasions."

As the two young women were passing a street crossing, they turned to their left and saw the ghost of Abraham Lincoln standing there. Rather than running off screaming, as some would have done, they posed several questions to the ghost, and each was answered to their satisfaction, though they refused to repeat any of the conversation.

"Very few citizens were disposed to believe it," wrote the paper, "but the young ladies declare upon their honor it was so, and being willing to testify to it, and the assertion of other parties, to the effect that they saw the girls standing at that particular place, gazing intently at something, has convinced many that there is something in it."[221]

To say that Mount Pleasant had any connection to Lincoln would be a stretch, but not a total stretch: the year before, in 1868, Abraham's son Robert had married Mary Harlan, a girl from Mount Pleasant, and Robert would often spend time in the city over the years. She gave birth to Lincoln's first grandchild only a few months after the encounter; one can speculate that the ghost might have wanted to see the town for himself. Not many hunts for Lincoln's ghost have taken place in Iowa since, though.

Perhaps the location outside of Washington, DC, with the best-sourced Lincoln ghost sightings is Fort Monroe, a former military installation in Hampton, Virginia, that remained in Union hands throughout the war, and has now become something of a ghost-hunting hot spot.

Few places in the world have a more impressive list of former guests than the old fort. Lincoln was a guest there several times during the war. Following the war, former President Jefferson Davis was imprisoned there for his supposed role in plotting the Lincoln assassination (of which he was entirely innocent). Before either of them set foot on the grounds, Edgar Allan Poe served there for a time during his own brief stint in the army. Others who lived or stayed there include Robert E. Lee, the Marquis de Lafayette, the King of Hawaii, Chief Black Hawk, Andrew Jackson, and others. Captain John Smith even stopped on the grounds—then known as Old Point Comfort—four hundred years ago and remarked that it was a fine place for a castle.

There are many ghosts reported around the Fort (indeed, it's one of those locations that seems to be turning into something of a ghost-hunting theme park today, now that the Army has vacated the premises) including several anonymous spectres of all ages that no one can positively identify. Soldiers even used to speak of a monster in the moat. But Davis, Lincoln, and Poe are all among those commonly said to haunt the place. Conversations between the three would be fascinating to hear.

However, the three ghosts don't seem to be haunting the same parts of the old fort. Davis, naturally, is said to haunt the stone prisons. Poe, having spent more time in more parts of the fort than the other two during his four-month stay, is seen in various places around (one wonders if he ever re-enacts his attempts to get kicked out of the army; it's said that he used to show up for drills wearing nothing but a hat), though he probably wouldn't have spent much time in the guest quarters where Lincoln is sighted.

We can at least say the stories weren't made up in recent years just to attract tourists. As early as 1972, Jane Polansky, author of *The Ghosts of Fort Monroe*, was writing that one set of quarters had doors that opened and closed of their own accord, along with a chair that rocked itself and a record player that worked without help from living hands.

She pinpointed Lincoln's ghost as appearing in a guest room that was, by 1972, known as The Lincoln Room. "Lincoln," she said, "is said to have been seen standing by the fireplace in a dressing gown, apparently deep in thought."[222]

At least in this case, we can trace Lincoln to having been in the location at one point in his life. But one of the more compelling earlier stories takes place at a spot where Lincoln never set foot at all, and ties into another compelling set of mysteries: the legend of the bloody dress worn by Clara Harris, who was sitting in the presidential box at Ford's Theatre when the president was shot.

The Bloody Dress: Ghosts and Mysteries

When the *Albany Daily Evening Times* published their 1872 account of the ghost of the Lincoln funeral train, it's doubtful that the night watchmen who told the story knew that Lincoln's ghost had apparently been seen in Albany before—or that a blood-stained dress from the assassination was still hanging in a closet outside of town.

When the Lincolns attended the performance of *Our American Cousin*, they had no intention of going alone. General Grant was supposed to come, but declined at the last minute. Their son Robert, freshly arrived home, just wanted to stay in bed. The Marquis de Chambrun, who had accompanied Lincoln on the riverboat and listened to him reading from *Macbeth*, declined because it seemed wrong to attend a theater on Good Friday. Noah Brooks, the reporter who was the best source of the "Mirror" story, was asked to come, but had a cold.

With all of these choices exhausted, the Lincolns invited Major Henry Rathbone and his fiance, Clara Harris, to attend the play with them. Rathbone, a twenty-eight-year-old soldier who had inherited a fortune when his father died, was the stepson of Ira Harris, who had taken over William Seward's seat in the Senate. Harris was Clara's father, meaning that the affianced couple also happened to be stepsiblings. Little notice was taken of this at the time. They were simply another popular Washington couple, holding off their engagement until Rathbone could return from the war. (Like Robert, he was in Washington for the moment, but still on active duty as of April 14, 1865).

The assassination that took place that night is only a part of the story—one could actually say that the box the foursome sat in was cursed. Of the five people who entered the box that night (counting Booth), three would be shot to death, and the other two would eventually be declared insane.

The presidential party was probably all chuckling at the play's biggest laugh line ("Well, I guess I know enough to turn you inside out, old gal—you sockdologizing old man trap.") when Booth crept in and made his move, firing his pistol at the president's head. Lincoln wouldn't formally expire for several hours, but his consciousness was lost instantly. We can take a small measure of comfort in thinking that not only did he never knew what hit him, his last feelings were of humor and mirth.

Rathbone recalled days later that Booth shouted the word "Freedom" (or something like it—in the confusion he wasn't really sure), as he made for the edge of the box. As Rathbone tried to grab the fleeing actor, Booth stabbed at him with a knife, going straight for his heart. Rathbone moved quickly enough that the knife only slashed his arm, a wound that spilled far more blood, by most accounts, than the president's own gunshot wound.

The assassination, with the presidential party looking on. Courtesy Library of Congress.

Major Rathbone was soon taken to a nearby hospital, and Clara accompanied the party across the street to the boarding house, sitting in a front room while the dying president was placed in the bed. She was still in her dress, and soaked in Rathbone's blood (and perhaps some of the president's, though this, as we'll see, is a bit of a mystery itself).

In the boarding house, Mrs. Lincoln was hysterical. Every time she looked at Clara's bloody dress, she would shriek, "My husband's blood! My dear husband's blood!" There was no way to explain to her that it was probably actually mostly Rathbone's blood.

Clara could never bear to throw the dress away, or even to have it cleaned, and after returning to her family's house near Albany, New York, she hung it in a closet, which she then ordered to be bricked up.

According to legend (it's said to have been recorded in a town history book), on April 14, 1866, the first anniversary of the assassination, she awoke in her room and beheld the ghost of Abraham Lincoln, sitting in a chair facing the bricked-up closet and laughing to himself, as though he were watching a play. He vanished the moment the clock struck midnight, and Clara hysterically ran to tell her family what she'd seen.

Naturally, they told her it was only a dream. But she wasn't the only one to see the ghost in the cottage.

The ghost was seen again around the turn of the century—this time by the governor of Massachusetts. According to legend, he spent a night in the cottage one time around 1900. He was on vacation, but troubled greatly by a big decision that he had to make as governor. Late in the night, as he slept, he dreamed that Lincoln appeared to him in the room, giving him the courage and wisdom he needed to make the right decision. He awoke fresh, confident, and feeling as though Lincoln himself had truly come to him and given him counsel, even though it was only dream.

Then he opened the closet, where he found the white dress, stained in Lincoln's actual blood.

The files of the local historical society,[223] tell the story in somewhat more detail.

A few years after the turn of the century, the governor of Massachusetts was visiting his cousin at Loudon Cottage, a ghostly manifestation appeared. The governor retired late one autumn night, after a large dinner. His mind was troubled about signing a bill that had just been passed by his state Legislature. He finally fell asleep, but wakened soon to see a ghostly Lincoln in the moonlight. As he reached for the light, he overturned a pile of books and the apparition vanished. One of the books overturned was a Bible. It fell open to a page containing the word, "Hew Honestly to the line; let the Lord take care of the chips," words Lincoln once used in a speech. The governor then closed the book and paced it on a table next to his bed, for he had received a message and his decision was made.

Both Clara's tale and the governor's are difficult to verify. If Clara did, in fact, see the ghost in 1866, it would probably be the first recorded Lincoln ghost sighting, though no early source on the story has been found. The governor's ghost story is similarly lacking in provenance. Two men—Winthrop Murray Crane and John L. Bates—held the office of governor of Massachusetts in the first few years after the turn of the twentieth century. I couldn't confirm that either of them ever spent a night in the cottage or that either ever claimed that the ghost of Lincoln ever gave him advice on an important decision.

Still, the story has many wonderful hallmarks of a good ghost story—the idea that Lincoln's very spirit could have come into town along with the blood and guts that were never washed away from the beautiful dress is the stuff of legends.

Whether she'd seen a ghost or not, Clara's story was only beginning. She and Major Rathbone were married in 1867, but Rathbone was said to be driven mad with guilt over not being able to stop Booth (though no one ever seriously claimed that he could have). While it's impossible to say for certain that the events of 1865 destroyed his mental health (some blamed dyspepsia), nothing in his later conduct suggests otherwise.

One grim Christmas Eve morning, 1883, when the couple was living in Germany, servants in their house heard a terrible commotion and found Clara lying dead of a gunshot wound, and Henry Rathbone slashing at himself with a knife. He had, it seems, re-enacted the night of the execution, murdering Clara just the way that Booth had murdered Lincoln, and was now trying to finish the job on himself, stabbing at himself just the way Booth had stabbed at him. He recovered from the knife wounds again, but spent the rest of his life in an asylum, finally dying there in 1911.

In an interview shortly after Henry murdered Clara, ex-Sen. Hamilton Harris, said, "My belief is that Rathbone was … insane when he killed his wife. He was one of the kindest men toward his wife and family that I ever knew." [224]

Later accounts say that some years later, the Rathbone's son retrieved the dress that had been stained with blood from the bricked-up closet and burned it, believing that it had cursed his family. This, along with the story that the dress was bricked up at all, is also seemingly impossible to verify.

However, it should be noted that trying to verify details about anything to do with Henry and Clara Rathbone is terribly frustrating. I could find no reliable copy of Clara's letter containing an oft-quoted line that the president's wound did not bleed externally (which is often quoted by people trying to verify relics of the assassination—dress fragments and such—that are said to be stained by Lincoln's own blood) and that Mrs. Lincoln thought the blood on the dress was Abraham's. A deposition Clara gave shortly after the assassination has survived, and there is a letter to a friend written two weeks later in circulation, but the actual text reads, "My dress is saturated with blood; my hands and face were covered. You may imagine what a scene! And so, all through that dreadful night, when we stood by that dying bed. Poor Mrs. Lincoln was and is almost crazy."[225] Comments on whose blood it was, or what Mrs. Lincoln thought of the sight, are absent from both the letter and the deposition.

Even what sort of outfits Clara and Henry wore to the theater is the subject of some controversy. Not only do we not know for certain that the dress was bricked up and later burned, we also have no idea what would have happened to it if that wasn't the case. We don't even know what sort of dress she was wearing, really. Though a fragment of sleeve lining said to be a part of Clara's dress is in a museum, that piece of sleeve lining is the only real clue—the dress itself was generally said to be of white satin, but that may simply be because it was described as such in a 1930 novel by Mary Raymond Shipman Andrews. Indeed, it's been suggested that a great deal of what we think we know about the couple at all really just comes from fiction. Stories about them that novelists made up are often mistakenly repeated as fact.

Rathbone's outfit is also a mystery. He was still on active duty in the military and, hence, generally depicted as wearing his uniform, but the only real indication we have that he was thus attired comes from Booth's diary, which mentions that "a colonel" was sitting in the booth near Lincoln. This diary was written some time later, when Booth may have read in papers that the Lincolns' guest was a military man. A couple of witnesses described the other man in the president's box wearing "citizen's clothes."

Truly, the story of Clara and Henry is a fine example of the difficulties of studying anything to do with Lincoln. For every piece of evidence, there's something to refute that evidence, and sometimes it seems like none of the hundred or so witnesses to the assassination saw the same event. There is debate about what Booth said, whether the actress Laura Keene cradled the president in her arms for a moment before he was moved, what everyone was wearing, how long Booth was in the presidential box, whether he caught his spur on a flag while jumping down, whether his leg was broken, and who actually carried Lincoln to the boarding house across the street (countless people visited the Peterson House in the late nineteenth and early twentieth century claiming to have been among the group that brought the wounded president across the street—far, far, more than could have actually done so). Nearly nothing about the night can be said without some qualifier or sidebar.

And one possible explanation as to why the minutely-studied event remains so cloudy and mysterious may be the strangest piece of Lincoln lore yet.

The Time Traveler's Tale

The photograph that follows shows the only confirmed image of Lincoln at Gettysburg on the day of his famous address—there're a couple of other crowd shots said to show even less distinct images of him, though they've never really been confirmed.

Little attention was ever paid to the boy in the foreground until 2004, when Seattle attorney Andrew Basiago began to say that the boy was him.

According to Basiago, as a child he was a part of a top-secret government project called Project Pegasus. As a participant, he used eight different time travel technologies that the government had discovered in the 1960s using ideas found on papers salvaged from Nikola Tesla's apartment.

He told the (naturally skeptical) *Huffington Post* that he traveled back to 1863 Gettysburg from 1972 New Jersey.

Lincoln is barely visible among the heads in the background at Gettysburg. Is there a chance that the kid in the foreground was a time traveler from the twentieth century? Library of Congress.

"I had been dressed in period clothing, as a Union bugle boy," he said. "I attracted so much attention at the Lincoln speech site at Gettysburg—wearing over-sized men's street shoes—that I left the area and walked about 100 feet over to where I was photographed."[226]

He also said that he traveled back to Ford's Theatre on April 14, 1865, several times, though he never actually saw the assassination—the closest he came was one trip when he was on the theater level and heard the gun shot.

Interestingly, Basiago claims that each time he went to the theater on the fateful night, the events he saw were slightly different, as though he was being sent to "slightly different alternative realities."

If we take a great leap and assume Basiago is telling the truth (which, just so we're clear, probably also requires us to assume he's telling the truth when he says that he and Barack Obama were sent on missions to Mars in the early 1980s, which a spokesman for the National Security Council actually went to the trouble of denying in 2012), there are a number of questions raised here. Would the same boy have been in those Gettysburg pictures before 1972, when Basiago made the jump? Are the books on our shelves changing every time someone from Project Pegasus, or some other time travel agency, changes something in the past?

And could it just be that the reason the accounts of what happened that night are different really is just that the event keeps getting changed slightly? Or that, on such a historic occasion, people living in various alternative timelines all somehow converged on the same spot?

After spending enough time tracing different sources and footnotes of Lincoln lore, the idea that we can chalk things up to time travelers and alternate realities starts to seem more and more appealing.

Ten

———

Ghosts of DC

On a 2006 episode of *The Office*, Steve Carell (in character as Michael Scott) noted that the Lincoln assassination had just recently become an acceptable subject for jokes and comedy. It had passed the "too soon" rule.

That "too soon" rule can often be applied to ghost stories just as well as it applies to jokes. Speaking about the ghost of someone who just died is generally considered bad form, and this may explain why so few people outside of spiritualist circles really wrote about Lincoln's ghost in the nineteenth century. Besides the story of the phantom train and the odd tale of him roaming around in Mount Pleasant, Iowa, the only ghost stories that can reliably be traced back to having been told in the nineteenth century are of him materializing in cabinets or taking control of mediums. If he was still walking the earth as a ghost, he was apparently quiet, at least when he wasn't participating in seances.

The White House in Lincoln's era. Courtesy Library of Congress.

This would change in the early twentieth century, when stories of Lincoln's ghost became a part of American folklore. That enough time had passed is one reason for the sudden spread of Lincoln ghost stories in the 1920s, but another was simply that fewer and fewer people were left who could speak of Lincoln as a living person. The last people to see him alive were almost all dead by World War I, and by the time of World War II only a small handful of those who had even seen his face in 1901 when the coffin was moved were still alive, let alone those few who had seen him alive in 1865.

In 1930, the *Boston Herald* wrote an article about Dr. Charles Leale, who was fresh out of medical school the night Lincoln was shot and was among those who treated him—he was still alive in 1930, though he was a very old man by then. The other known people who had seen Lincoln in the flesh were a quickly dying breed—Jackson C. Taylor, a former slave who had been in the theater that night, had died just months before. Just before that, William J. Ferguson, the last survivor of the cast performing in the theater that night, had passed away.

Of people besides Dr. Leale who had been involved on the night of the assassination, Col. O. H. Oldroyd, who directed the Lincoln Museum in the Peterson House (where the president died), said, "There may be, probably are, still living a few persons who were in the audience that night, and perhaps a few who witnessed aftermath incidents of the assassination, such as the removal of the president to this house. But I know positively of none, although a member of the Garrett family, in whose Virginia barn Booth was captured, was still living a few years ago. Even the long procession of men who said they helped carry Mr. Lincoln from the theatre seems to have ended. We haven't heard in several years a living claimant to that distinction…no one who was around the theatre that night ever drops in here now, as many of them used to."[227]

Perhaps the growth in Lincoln ghostlore in the twentieth century came about simply because, with new stories about seeing Lincoln in the flesh dying away, fresh stories about Lincoln could only be stories of his spirit. In the twentieth century, the ghost was most commonly reported—by far—at the White House.

Abraham isn't the only Lincoln ghost who is seen there—there have been vague stories of Willie Lincoln making his presence known in the room where he died, though few have given details, except for Lynda Johnson Robb, Lyndon B. Johnson's daughter, who lived in Willie's room and was "very much aware" that Willie had died where she was sleeping. Stories abound that members of the Grant administration saw Willie Lincoln's ghost in the White House in the 1860s and 1870s, but, again, details are scarce. All I could ever find were some offhand mentions from the 1950s.

The White House certainly seems as though it *ought* to be haunted, though. Besides Willie Lincoln, several people have died in the executive mansion, including Presidents William Henry Harrison and Zachary Taylor, as well as two nineteenth-century First Ladies, President Grant's father-in-law, and a diplomat from Hawaii who collapsed and died in a hallway during the Chester A. Arthur administration.[228]

The first witness to the ghost of Abraham Lincoln himself in the White House is often said to be Theodore Roosevelt, though his own comments were clearly supposed to be metaphorical, not literal. The story of his sighting can be traced to a letter he wrote to Dr. Henry S. Pritchett on December 14, 1904: "I think of Lincoln, shambling, homely, with his strong, sad, deeply furrowed face, all the time. I see him in the different rooms and in the halls. For some reason or other he is to me infinitely the most real of the dead presidents. So far as one who is not a great man can model himself on one who was, I try to follow out the general lines of policy which Lincoln laid down."[229]

This is sort of emblematic of how most reported White House ghost sightings work. Though there have been countless articles and books full of presidential ghost stories, many of those that can be traced to anything at all simply go back to one simple comment that's been taken out of context. No one had yet reported Lincoln's ghost in the White House in Theodore Roosevelt's time, so far as is known, and seen in full, Roosevelt's own quote is clearly not a sighting of the ghost, just a quote about how strongly Lincoln affected his imagination. It would be some time yet before there was a proper Lincoln ghost sighting; in the fifteen years or so after Roosevelt left office, White House staff and residents would speak mainly about the ghosts of Dolly Madison and Abigail Adams.

Of course, this is only going by what was actually written down. There's no telling how long stories of Lincoln's ghost had been a part of oral tradition among White House workers and residents by the time they began circulating outside of the gates. The first known sighting of Lincoln's ghost is often attributed to Grace Coolidge, wife of president Calvin Coolidge, but from the context of the known sightings, it's clear that the story of the ghost seemed to be well known by then.

Every newcomer to the White House in Coolidge's day was told of a legend that whenever the light over the front door of the White House was dimmed for the evening, the ghost of Lincoln would pace silently across the North Porch.[230] It's often said that Grace Coolidge once claimed in a newspaper article that she herself had once seen Lincoln's apparition standing at the window in the Oval Office, dressed all in black, with a stole over his shoulders "to ward off the drafts and chills of Washington's night air."[231]

I couldn't locate the original article, but that Grace Coolidge claimed to have seen the ghost was part of White House oral tradition by the Truman era a generation later, when nearly everyone asked about ghosts in the White House would say that they'd heard that the former First Lady had once encountered the phantom. But it was really during the Franklin D. Roosevelt era that the sightings became most common.

Lincoln's Ghost in the Franklin D. Roosevelt Era

In 1954, Eleanor Roosevelt was asked about ghosts in the White House by reporter Leslie Lieber. Lieber expected her to decline to discuss the subject, but the former First Lady was actually happy to share what she knew.

"Ghost scare?" she said. "Yes, you might say we had one shortly after we moved into the White House. It was in 1934. There was a member of the staff named Mary. One afternoon she went to the second floor. She couldn't have been up there more than three minutes, but when she ran downstairs she was terribly wrought up. She gasped that she had just seen Abraham Lincoln seated on his bed, pulling on his boots."[232]

Asked if she'd ever had a ghostly encounter of her own, Eleanor said, "It's the same thing in all creaky old houses. If you're prowling around late at night, you get a feeling that 'someone is there.' Old-timers in the White House are more conscious of Lincoln than of any other past president because each room he used is marked by a plaque. My own sitting room had been his bedroom. Sometimes when I worked at my desk I'd get a feeling that someone was standing behind me. Sometimes I'd have to turn around and look."[233]

Skeptical though she was, Mrs. Roosevelt did relate an incident about Carl Sandburg, the poet and Lincoln biographer (who had cleaned up the story of Austin Gollaher's hat by saying that young Lincoln had tried to drop a "paw paw" fruit into it in his biography). One night, Sandburg and President Roosevelt fell into a chat about Lincoln, speculating about which rooms he had used to write certain letters. They wandered into the Oval Room, the room where Sandburg had always imagined Lincoln working. "While Franklin sat meditating in silence," Eleanor said, "Sandburg stood quietly at the window that faces the Potomac Flats—the very window where Lincoln often stood during the Civil War, moodily gazing toward the front in Virginia. For fully ten minutes, Mr. Sandburg looked out into the distance…Then, suddenly, he turned around and, with great finality, said 'Mr. President, this is the room.'"

Mrs. Roosevelt also noted that "in the past half century," several employees had reported seeing Lincoln's ghost staring out of that same window.

John Mays, the doorman for several decades, was also interviewed for Lieber's article (which became the source of a great deal of White House ghostlore, though it's seldom credited) and seemed to be a veritable font of stories. He told a tale that one day, President Roosevelt's valet "ran out of here … into the arms of a guard, shouting that he had just seen Lincoln."

The valet was tracked down by Lieber and Mays, but he didn't wish to speak at first, saying he didn't suppose that the current president, Dwight D. Eisenhower, would like it if he knew that he was living in a haunted house. He eventually agreed to speak only on the condition of anonymity, and claimed that one night, a very famous woman (suspected by the editor of Lieber's article of having been Queen Wilhelmina of the Netherlands, though it could also have been her daughter, Princess Juliana, or someone else entirely) was staying in the Rose Room of the White House. "One evening," he said, "the butler and I were serving cocktails to the guest and the president. The great lady turned to Mr. Roosevelt and made the startling announcement that she had fainted the night before. The president was shocked and asked what had happened. 'Someone knocked on my door in the middle of the night,' she said. 'I got up and opened it and—I know this sounds ridiculous—but I saw Abraham Lincoln standing there. Then everything went black and I came to on the floor.'"

*Queen Wilhelmina in 1942, when she is said to have seen
Lincoln's ghost during a visit to the White House.
Courtesy Library of Congress.*

Though it couldn't be confirmed or denied that Queen
Wilhelmina was actually the witness in question, she's been
confidently said to have had an encounter with the ghost
ever since. During her visit in 1942, the queen addressed
an incredibly rare joint meeting of Congress, but it was her
supposed meeting with the ghost that is generally remembered today. Nearly nothing else about her time in Washington is ever written about now. We do, at least, know that

both the queen and her daughter stayed in the Rose Room, often spoken of as a hotbed of ghost sightings.

The valet wasn't the only staffer of the nameless valet's era with ghost stories to tell. Lillian Rogers Park, a maid and seamstress in the White House at the time, spoke freely of ghosts in the White House in her 1961 book, *Backstairs at the White House*, specifying that Lincoln was most often seen in the Oval Room, looking out at the view that went all the way to Virginia, as he often did in life.

Parks had ghostly encounters of her own. One day, while preparing a bed for the visiting Queen Elizabeth, she felt that something was looking at her. She perceived "something coldish" behind her, but couldn't bring herself to look.[234]

She also spoke of another staff member hearing loud, hollow laughter coming from the Rose Room on the second-floor and finding that no one was there. The room had been a room for presidential secretaries in Lincoln's day. Another employee, Katurah Brooks, told Leslie Lieber that she, too, had heard a burst of laughter—"loud and booming, like out of a cavern"—coming from the bed. Neither thought it was Lincoln—the bed in the room at the time had belonged to Andrew Jackson.[235]

Another time during the Roosevelt era, Parks was putting a room together that contained Lincoln's bed and kept hearing footsteps going through the larger room, which held the bed, and coming up toward the door to the smaller adjacent room where she was working. She looked up again and again and found no one there. After some time, she asked a houseman who had kept walking across the Lincoln Bedroom without coming in.

"I just came on duty," the houseman said. "That was Abe you heard."

"He was," Parks wrote, "perfectly serious."[236]

Perhaps the most famous story of a ghost sighting in the Roosevelt years concerns Winston Churchill, who spent a few weeks at the White House around Christmas, 1941. The story may merely have started with the tale that Churchill refused to stay in Lincoln's bedroom, a fact which may have at least a kernel of truth behind it. J. B. West, the chief usher, wrote that President Roosevelt had arranged for Churchill to stay in the Lincoln room initially. "However," wrote West, "he didn't like the bed, so he tried out all the beds and finally selected the rose suite at the east end of the second floor."[237]

*Winston Churchill, fully dressed, at the White House
in 1929. Courtesy Library of Congress.*

It was probably not the ghosts that kept him out of the room, as is sometimes said, but even if it was, legend has it that the move didn't save him from ghosts. The best of the Churchill ghost stories is too wonderful not to retell, despite a general lack of source: according to legend, one night Churchill was taking a bath in the Lincoln bedroom, and wandered out of the tub—butt naked—and saw Abraham Lincoln standing in the room, smiling softly.

"Mr. President!" said Prime Minister Churchill. "You seem to have me at a disadvantage."

The ghost of Lincoln smiled, then vanished like a breath into the wind.

I dearly wish I could back this one up with primary sources, or even secondary ones, but Churchill never seems to have told the story himself, and I couldn't find any reference to him seeing Lincoln's ghost in print at all from before the 1970s. Like Lincoln himself, Churchill is the subject of many colorful anecdotes that probably never happened, and has many delightful, pithy quotes that are attributed to him despite the fact that he never said anything of the sort. Furthermore, it's simply unlikely, based on J. B. West's memories of Churchill, that he would have referred to being naked in front of a ghost as a disadvantage.

"The staff," West said, "did have a little difficulty in adjusting to Mr. Churchill's way of living. We got used to his 'jumpsuit,' the one-piece uniform he wore every day, but the servants never quite got over seeing him naked in his room when they'd go up to serve brandy. It was the jumpsuit or nothing. In his room, Mr. Churchill wore no clothes at all most of the time during the day."[238]

Harry Truman: Ghost Tour Guide

By the time Harry Truman moved into the White House with his family in 1945, he went around with J. B. West, the usher trying to figure out what to do with each room. Eventually, they came to the Lincoln room, which featured "massive Victorian furniture" and an enormous bed. Truman paused and said, "Would we dare move Mr. Lincoln out of here, or would we be tampering with history too much?"

"Well, I'm sure Mr. Lincoln probably slept in every room in the house," said West. "Actually, the room that Mrs. Truman has chosen for her sitting room was probably where Lincoln slept. The Coolidges kept the Lincoln furniture there, and President and Mrs. Coolidge slept in the room together. The Hoovers slept in the same room, but they moved the Lincoln furniture across the hall to where it is now. You could just as easily move it down the hall over to the East Room, because that was the Lincoln Cabinet Room, where he signed the Emancipation Proclamation."

"Now I know why they say Lincoln's ghost walks around up here at night," Truman said. "He's just looking for his bed."[239]

Truman loved the sense of history behind the White house. "There are so many memories here," he said to West. "Why, I can almost believe in Lincoln's ghost myself." However, by the time he moved in, the old house had fallen into such disrepair that the tub in his bathroom was sinking into the floor. He warned his wife that some afternoon when she was hosting a Daughters of the American Revolution tea downstairs, the tub might come crashing through—with him inside. She didn't think it was as funny as he did.

Eventually, President Truman and his family moved out of the main residence so repairs and renovations could be made. When the work was nearly done in 1952, Truman took reporters on a White House tour, telling them that he was anxious to get back into his residence, not least because he wanted to get back to looking for Lincoln's ghost. After the tour, it was his ghost stories that everyone remembered and wrote about. While showing reporters around the almost-completed renovations, he said that "White House servants for years have borne testimony to nocturnal strolls by Lincoln's ghost through the upstairs halls."[240]

On May 27, 1955, Margaret Truman, the now-former president's daughter, substituted for Edward R. Murrow as the host of his TV show, *Person to Person*, and hosted a folksy chat with her parents on the porch of the Missouri home to which they'd moved after leaving office in 1953. Before a national audience, Truman spoke a bit about the mysterious footsteps he would hear in the White House from time to time. "I think it's the ghost of Abraham Lincoln walking around," he said. "Perhaps there to warn me about something."[241]

He also spoke of having been disturbed by tapping sounds at his door—"unusually sad and melancholy" taps, usually around three a.m. He'd open the door and find nothing but darkness. He blamed it, perhaps not entirely seriously, on Lincoln's ghost, possibly walking the halls, trying to express his concern over the rising East-West tensions between the United States and Russia that then threatened to tear the world apart just as North-South tensions did in his own day. Of course, the house was falling apart at the time, and he specified on the air that it only really happened before the house was repaired.

He also let Margaret in on a secret (which she apparently didn't know, though Truman had told the story to reporters in 1952), that one day, when she and her friends had held a sleepover in Lincoln's old bed, he had thought about playing a prank on her. He had asked one of the staff to dress up as Lincoln and give them all a good scare. Mrs. Truman had vetoed the plan.[242] His diary gives the date for this trick as having been exactly ten years before, on May 27, 1945.

For her part, Margaret wrote the next year about the Lincoln bed ("lumpy!") and said, "I don't know why I wanted to sleep in Lincoln's bed, except that there was a legend around the White House that Lincoln's shadow sometimes reappeared in his room. The maids and butlers were always claiming that he came back." She had enlisted two friends to join her out of sheer nervousness, but they found themselves unable to sleep in the old bed. Not due to the ghosts—like Churchill, they simply found it terribly uncomfortable, though they tried positioning themselves "up and down, lengthwise, cross-wise, and catawampus."[243]

There is some confusion as to why Truman's planned prank didn't happen. Truman blamed his wife when he told the story on the TV show, but both Margaret and J. B. West wrote that the man Truman had picked to dress up as Lincoln, John Mays (the same doorman who had told the story of Roosevelt's valet seeing the ghost) didn't feel right about it and called in sick. It may also be worth noting that at twenty-one, Margaret would have been a bit old for this sort of prank).

The Lincoln bedroom, with the bed on the left, as it appeared in June 1960. Abraham probably never used the bed himself, though Willie died in it. Barbara Bush replaced the mattress, but it's still said to be lumpy. Courtesy Robert Knudsen, White House Photographs, John F. Kennedy Presidential Library and Museum, Boston.

Truman had spoken of the knockings and footsteps before—Leslie Lieber (the same reporter who spoke to Eleanor Roosevelt) had asked them about them the year before after reading his diary entry about the planned prank. He told her that he had first heard stories of ghosts in the White House from the barber there, and that staff members who were "attuned to such things" often insisted that they could hear Lincoln pacing the floors. When asked if he'd seen anything ghostly himself, he quickly pointed out that old houses tended to creak and make noise, but admitted that on one or two occasions during the war, he'd been awakened by the sound of a knock at his door. Thinking that it was someone telling him that Winston Churchill was phoning from London, he'd run to the door. But when he opened it, he found nothing but darkness.[244]

Lincoln's Ghost at the White House in the 1960s and 1970s

After the busy years of the Roosevelt and Truman administrations, things largely quieted down for the next several administrations, though minor sightings continued to be mentioned in books and articles from time to time.

Liz Carpenter, Lyndon B. Johnson's press secretary, told author John Alexander that she thought that Lady Bird, the First Lady, had seen Lincoln's ghost—or felt his presence, in any case. One April night in the 1960s, Lady Bird was watching a TV show about Lincoln's death (likely around the one hundredth anniversary in April 1965). "Suddenly," Carpenter said, "she was aware, conscious of the fact, that the room she was in was special. Someone was compelling her eyes toward the mantel."

On the mantel was one of the plaques about Lincoln's doings in the room that Eleanor Roosevelt had spoken of—one that Lady Bird hadn't noticed before. As she read it, Carpenter said, "She felt a chill. A draft."[245]

Some years later, in 1971, Julie Nixon, the daughter of then president Richard Nixon, was giving blind children a tour of the White House, she took them to the Lincoln bedroom and, after pointing out that Lincoln hadn't actually slept in this room, and then finding out how many of them could fit into the bed at once (thirteen), she told them the story of Queen Wilhelmina's encounter with Lincoln's ghost. Asked by a reporter if she'd seen the ghost herself, she said that while some told stories of "thumpings," she had not. "I've never seen a ghost, I've never heard a ghost," she said.[246]

The next president's daughter, Susan Ford, didn't see the ghost, either, but partly because she didn't want to look. She told reporters that she believed in ghosts, and that was why she had no intention of sleeping in Lincoln's bed, even though J. B. West had once said that sleeping in Lincoln's old bed was one thing that every presidential family just had to do. Ford wrote in her column in *Seventeen* magazine that many people had seen the ghost, and she didn't want to be the next one.[247]

The Ford family only seems to have had one brief, not-completely serious scare: when they moved into the White House, they heard strange clicking sounds that they said (presumably with a smile) were the sound of Lincoln's ghost. They were actually the sound of clicking billiard balls on a pool table someone had given to Richard Nixon. Mrs. Ford put down carpet to muffle the sound.[248]

The ghost, indeed, seemed quiet for much of the 1960s and 1970s. Amy Carter, daughter of President Jimmy Carter, apparently once tried to contact Lincoln with a Ouija board with some friends during a White House sleepover, but the ghost wasn't talkative that night even when he was called.

Reagan- and Bush-Era Ghosts

After this quiet period, the ghost of Lincoln seemed to make a comeback in the 1980s, during the Reagan administration. In 2003, a video on the whitehouse.gov website featured White House operations foreman Tony Savoy telling a story about a day in the early 1980s when he was working on the second floor, flipped on a switch in a room of the residence, and saw Lincoln' ghost, dressed in a pinstripe suit and sitting in a chair, his hands folded together and his legs crossed. The vision was gone after Savoy blinked his eyes.[249]

Though Ronald Reagan himself never saw the ghost of Lincoln, he made several jokes about it, and had many occasions to do so—a few members of his family did claim to see the ghost, starting with Rex the dog. His wife, Nancy, told reporters about it in February 1986, while standing next to an eight-foot-high wooden valentine sent to her by 1950s-era teen idol Bobby Vinton—an odd place to tell an odd ghost story.

"Rex will go barking down the hall," Nancy Reagan said, "and my husband said, 'I'll bet he senses Abe is here.'" Asked if she believed the story, she said, "I don't know. Do you?"[250]

Months later, when told that a house he'd be staying in overseas was haunted, President Reagan said, "We've got a couple of ghosts here!"[251]

The next year, *Newsweek* did a whole story on the Lincoln ghost, and Nancy denied seeing any ghosts herself. "If Ronnie is away for a night or something, I can be here alone," she said. "I'm not afraid. I don't hear Abe Lincoln knocking on my door."

But her daughter Maureen Reagan said that she had seen the apparition personally. "I'm not kidding," she said. "We've really seen it." She and her husband, Dennis Revell, slept in Lincoln's old bed when they visited (uncomfortable though it was, it was the only bed in which Dennis could fit—he was six-foot-seven), an "aura" would appear in the late hours of the night, sometimes in red, sometimes in orange. Maureen, who was known to be a bit eccentric, believed—or at least half-believed—that it was Lincoln's ghost.

"When I told my parents what I saw," Maureen told *Newsweek*, "They looked at me a little weirdly."

In her memoir *My Turn*, Nancy Reagan spoke a bit about Maureen's story, expanding the tale a bit to say it was Dennis who saw the ghost first—a shadowy figure standing by the fireplace. Maureen, she said, laughed at Dennis, until she saw it herself one night, in the form of a translucent figure in a red coat. He was looking out the window, but turned and looked at her before vanishing.

"When Ronnie heard these stories," she wrote, "he just laughed them off. 'If you see him again,' he told Maureen, 'why don't you send him down the hall? I've got a few questions I'd like to ask him.'"

She further noted that one day when she straightened a picture in the Lincoln bedroom, a maid said "Oh, he's been here again." "Most of the White House staff seemed to believe in Lincoln's ghost," she wrote, "and they told stories of Eisenhower and Churchill both seeing him. Who's to say? But if he is there, I wish I could have seen him before we left."[252]

Early in her own stay in the White House, Barbara Bush, the next First Lady after Nancy Reagan, said she was sure that if there was a ghost, she and President Bush's dog, Millie, would know. Eventually, she wrote in her own 1995 memoir that, "I think we were aware of Lincoln's presence more than any of our other predecessors…However, we never saw or believed in the famous ghost, nor did (the dogs) Ranger and Millie."

On Halloween 1997, the story of Lincoln's ghost was revived one more time, when staffers from the Clinton White House spoke a bit about the ghosts. "A high percentage of people who work here won't go in the Lincoln bedroom," said Capricia Marshall, the social secretary. During her time in the White House, there had been an usher who went into the room to turn the lights out, and when he walked away, they had turned themselves back on again."

By then, though, most of the ghost stories among the staff seemed to revolve around the ghost of Preston, a White House doorman who died while still employed. When asked if she believed in the stories, Marshall merely said, "They're fun."[253]

First Lady Hillary Clinton was asked about the ghosts the same year on *The Rosie O'Donnell Show*, and her comments were similar to Eleanor Roosevelt's. She said, "There's something about the White House at night. You just feel like you're summoning up the spirits of all the people who've lived there and worked there and walked through the halls there. It ... can be a little creepy. You know, they think there's a ghost."

Clinton said she didn't believe in the ghost herself, but mentioned that one of her friends refused to sleep in the Lincoln bedroom due to the ghost stories.[254]

So ...

Is Abraham Lincoln haunting the White House? With so many first-hand accounts—far more than any other White House ghost (or most any other ghost anywhere)—it's certainly tempting to imagine so.

Think of the theories that intense mental energy can create a ghostly "imprint" on the environment. And then imagine Lincoln staring out the window, across the Potomac to Virginia, the Confederacy, as his ghost is often said to do.

I particularly think of the day very early in the war, when Lincoln could see a Confederate flag raised up over a hotel across the river. E. C. Ellsworth had lately commanded a drill team, the Zouaves, that made him one of the most famous men in the country. After the Zouaves national tour, Ellsworth had then taken a job in Lincoln's Springfield office and become something of a son to Lincoln (one he got along with better than Robert). Following him to the White House, he saw the flag and promised to capture it personally at once.

Leading a small band into the Confederacy, the flag was taken down, but Ellsworth was killed by the hotel owner in the process. It was, by some measures, the first Union combat casualty of the war, and Ellsworth became a national hero, with streets named after him in towns all over. Lincoln is said to have mourned him like a son. One can also imagine that perhaps Ellsworth was the soldier who died "in defense of the old flag" and now made pianos tilt at the Laurie's house. One can imagine Lincoln looking out his window at that hotel, wondering how many more sons would be lost.

Could it be that Lincoln's anguish and grief have left behind an imprint that some people picked up on when they stood in those spots decades later?

Or could it just be those little plaques Eleanor Roosevelt spoke of playing with everyone's head?

Decades have gone by in between sightings of the ghost, but as long as Lincoln continues to haunt our national consciousness, it's unlikely that we'll stop hearing reports of his ghost. Either figuratively or literally, it's safe to assume that Abraham Lincoln will be haunting us for a long time to come.

Conclusion

I sometimes think our era will be a boring one to study. It isn't that nothing interesting is happening, it's just that everything is so well documented now that it'll take some of the fun out of it. Lincoln lived in perhaps the most entertaining era to examine: the fact that we don't know exactly what Lincoln sounded like, among other mysteries about him, keeps the work interesting, but the growth of photography and newspapers gives us a lot of material to wade through. You can spend all day just reading newspaper accounts of what went on in Congress the day the House of Representatives passed the Thirteenth Amendment. And those old papers are addictive, because they're a fascinating glimpse into an era so different from our own that it's hard to comprehend what people could have been thinking at the time.

Abraham Lincoln, taken in November 1863.
Courtesy Library of Congress.

But you at least get a good idea of what was on their minds.

The sighting of the meteor of 1860 in Chattanooga, Tennessee, for instance, appeared in the fourth column on the first page of the September 27, *Charleston Mercury*.

The first column, as usual, was advertisements.

The second began with a paragraph quoted from a New Orleans paper stating that "Southern slavery, as a rule, is the mildest and most benevolent system of labor in the world, and the slaves, without abolition temptation, are the most happy and contented laborers. It is...in comparison with Abolitionism...most saintly and holy."

The next paragraph spoke of "the doom which Benedict Arnold escaped" (being hanged) and recommended the same fate for William Seward, Horace Greeley, Charles Sumner, and their abettors. "Shame on the ignoble souls who thus attempt to weaken the public confidence in reference to the monstrous iniquity of abolition!" the paper roared. It then had a few choice words for Lincoln and his "Black Republicans," assuring readers that they planned to overthrow slavery.

The next article down was a brief quote from Judge B. H. Hill. After stating that the Douglas Democrats and the John Bell "Constitutional Union" party members were "in love with each other and gazing at the moon together," despite the fact that they were running against each other for president, Hill said that if Douglas was elected, it would be "a declaration that there is no government for the slaveholder." And this is Douglas they were talking about. The guy who argued for slavery against Lincoln.

From there the second column went into some talk about consumption (tuberculosis) and rumors that a massive steam-powered printing press was being built in New York, though by the end of the column they were back to saying that if Lincoln were elected, the southern states should secede, and a report that a mob in the north had attacked a marshal who was trying to enforce the Fugitive Slave Law.

Now, keep in mind, this is just one random day in the *Charleston Mercury*. Similar rhetoric appeared all over in southern papers, and had for years by 1860. When people tell me that slavery had little to do with the South seceding, I wonder if they've ever read an issue of these old papers.

Lincoln had been, honestly, downright wishy-washy on slavery and black rights throughout the 1850s, suggesting nothing harsher than that he wished to halt slavery's spread and that he hoped it died out eventually. By the time of his second inaugural, though, after years of fierce fighting and hundreds of thousands dead, the South's worst fears had been realized. He had pushed the Thirteenth Amendment, outlawing slavery, through Congress, and it was only a matter of time before the states ratified it.

Lincoln didn't do it alone; there were countless soldiers, statesmen, and ordinary citizens who helped in ways big and small. Even his enemies did their part—without Stephen Douglas helping to grow Chicago into a city that could hold a major convention (when it had been a mud hole only twenty years before), Lincoln likely never would have been nominated at all. But whether the feat of bringing slavery to an end could have been done as early as it was with anyone else steering the ship of state is debatable, at the very least.

Always playing chess while others were demanding that he play checkers, Lincoln proved them all wrong in the end. By spring of 1865, even the *Charleston Mercury* was sort of in awe of him. They still hated his guts, but they envied that the northern states had such a brilliant leader while they were stuck with Jefferson Davis. Back in Chicago, Wilbur Storey's copperhead *Times* was at least saying that Lincoln had gotten better lately, and was commending his taste in music,[255] which was pretty high praise, considering the source.

Then, in an instant, at his moment of triumph, Lincoln was gone.

Lincoln's career is stunning to look at, really. With southern states looking as though they might finally be ready to make good on the secession threats they'd been making for years, the country was facing its darkest hour in 1860, and the people elected a folksy small-town rail-splitter to lead them through it.

Though there had been a couple of presidents of humble origin by then, Lincoln was not a famous war hero, had never been a governor or a big shot in Congress. He had almost no formal education, was not a member of any church, and his political party hadn't even existed a few years before. That a man with such a background could be nominated today seems utterly unbelievable, and would have seemed so then, too. To put their faith in such an unknown person at such a critical juncture almost seems reckless of the voters.

The mid-1800s were a strange time that called for strange solutions.

It was only fitting that we'd be left with strange stories to tell.

Acknowledgments

*R*esearch for this book has been rather exhausting; in an age when more and more information is available, I strongly believe that ghost and paranormal fans deserve better than what they've been getting. Many organizations have made information available that helped me greatly, but among the most important were:

- The defunct Chicago newspapers microfilm collection at the Harold Washington Public Library

- Genealogy Bank

- The International Association for the Preservation of Spiritualist and Occult Periodicals

- The DePaul University Library
- The Abraham Lincoln Papers at the Library of Congress
- *Chicago Tribune* archives via Chicago Public Library
- College of Psychic Studies, London
- archive.org
- Project Gutenberg

Endnotes

1. Richard Sheil, *The Apostate: A Tragedy in Five Acts as Performed at the Chestnut Street Theatre* (Philadelphia: Nbal and Mackenzie, 1828).

2. "Theatrical," *Chicago Tribune*, January 29, 1862.

3. Abraham Lincoln to James Hackett, August 17, 1863, http://memory.loc.gov/cgi-bin/query/P?mal:1:./temp/~ammem_uNP7

4. Adolphe de Pineton Chambrun, "Personal Recollections of Mr. Lincoln," *The Century Magazine*, 1893.

5. Charles Sumner, *Memoirs and Letters of Charles Sumner* (Boston: Roberts Brothers, 1893).

6. Karen Roach, "Lincoln Ghost Haunted Loudonville," *Schenectady Gazette*, October 31, 1989.

7. J. Rogers Gore, *The Boyhood of Abraham Lincoln from the Spoken Narratives of Austin Gollaher* (Indianapolis, IN: Bobbs-Merrill Co., 1921).

8. Douglas Wilson, "Charles Friend to William H. Herndon" in *Herndon's Informants: Letters, Interviews, and Statements about Abraham Lincoln* (Urbana, IL: University of Illinois Press, 1998).

9. William Herndon, *Herndon's Lincoln: The True Story of a Great Life* (Springfield, IL: The Herndon's Lincoln Publishing Company, 1888).

10. ibid.

11. ibid.

12. J. Rogers Gore, *The Boyhood of Abraham Lincoln from the Spoken Narratives of Austin Gollaher* (Indianapolis, IN: Bobbs-Merrill Co., 1921).

13. ibid.

14. Douglas Wilson, "Joseph Gillespie to William Herndon, January 31, 1866," collected in *Herndon's Informants: Letters, Interviews, and Statements about Abraham Lincoln* (Urbana: University of Illinois Press, 1998).

15. Max Ehrmann, "Lincoln's Visit to Terre Haute," *Indiana Magazine of History,* March 1936.

16. Abraham Lincoln to J. W. Fell, December 20, 1859.

17. Quoted here from Daniel Wheeler, *Abraham Lincoln* (New York: MacMillan, 1921).

18. Clifton Nichols, *Life of Abraham Lincoln* (Crowell and Kirkpatrick, 1896).

19. John Hanks to Jesse Weik, April 19, 1888.

20. William Herndon, *Herndon's Lincoln: The True Story of a Great Life* (Springfield, IL: The Herndon's Lincoln Publishing Company, 1888).

21. *Buffalo Courier*, July 21, 1860.

22. Zella Armstrong, *The History of Hamilton County and Chattanooga, Tennessee,* Volume 1 (Chattanooga, TN: The Lookout Publishing Co., 1931).

23. "Letter from a Tourist, Look Out Mountain House Near Chattanooga, TN, August 1860," *Charleston Mercury* (Charleston, SC), September 27, 1860.

24. *Chicago Times*, quoted in *The Constitution* (Washington, DC), August 18, 1860.

25. Editorial credited to "Rip Van Winkle," *Boston Herald,* July 30, 1860.

26. *Sacramento Union* quoted in "More About the Meteor," *New York Herald,* July 24, 1860.

27. Speech of Hon. Stephen A. Douglas on Measures of Adjustment, Delivering in the City Hall, Chicago, October 23, 1850. (New York: Jared W. Bell, 1851).

28. The new jail and criminal court buildings, where nearly 100 men would be hanged and where such criminals as Leopold and Loeb would later be tried, was built on the site of the "melee."

29. "The North Side: It Rejoices in a Public Building," *Chicago Tribune,* February 16, 1874.

30. "Border Ruffian Sexton Robbing Graves," *Chicago Tribune*, November 9, 1857.

31. Lincoln letter to Jesse Fell, printed in 1859 newspapers.

32. L. B. Taylor, *The Ghosts of Fredericksburg* (Williamsburg, VA: Progress Printing Company, 1991). the story is alluded to in some earlier sources

33. Herndon, William. "Letter from Lincoln's Old Law Partner," *Religion-Philosophical Journal*, December 12, 1885.

34. Noah Brooks, "Recollections of Abraham Lincoln," *Harper's New Monthly Magazine, Volume XXXI,* June–November, 1865.

35. Ward Hill Lamon, edited by Dorothy Lamon Teillard. *Recollections of Abraham Lincoln.* "Published by the Editor" Washington, DC, 1911.

36. Hans Holzer, *Famous Ghosts (*New York: Black Dog and Leventhal, 2012).

37. Ward Hill Lamon, *The Life of Abraham Lincoln, from His Birth to His Inauguration as President* (Boston: James R. Osgood and Co., 1872).

38. Augustus Chapman to William Herndon, October 8, 1865.

39. Ward Hill Lamon, *The Life of Abraham Lincoln, from His Birth to His Inauguration as President* (Boston: James R. Osgood and Co., 1872).

40. Douglas L. Wilson, ed.; Rodney O. Davis, ed.; Sarah Bush Lincoln, "Sarah Bush Lincoln" (William H. Herndon Interview). *Herndon's Informants: Letters, Interviews, and Statements About Abraham Lincoln* (Urbana: University of Illinois Press, 1998).

41. ibid.

42. *Herndon's Lincoln.*

43. "By Telegraph—Effects of Mr. Lincoln's Philadelphia Speech," *New York Commercial Advertiser*, February 21, 1862.

44. Ward Hill Lamon, edited by Dorothy Lamon Teillard. *Recollections of Abraham Lincoln.* "Published by the Editor," Washington, DC, 1911.

45. Isaac Newton Arnold, *Life of Abraham Lincoln.* McClurg and Co, Chicago, 1885.

46. George Ashmun to Isaac N. Arnold, October 16, 1864, reprinted in the *Springfield Republican*, October 26, 1864.

47. "The Rebel Gen. Lee," *New York Times* August 6, 1861. The letter also appeared in *The Macon Telegraph* and other publications that week, though it didn't appear in a book until the 1930s. No one seems to have questioned its authenticity, as it does sound like the sort of thing Lee would say (in an era when his persona wasn't as well known), but it seems odd to me that his most eloquent explanation for the side he chose was in a letter to a young admirer who asked for his photograph.

48. Some versions of the quote about "our national sins" contain an accurate prediction that "if it comes to a conflict of arms, the war will last at least four years," but that part is absent from the copies of the letter I found. According to a number of 1870s books, Lee's "four years" prediction allegedly came from an interview a "gentleman of New York" working on behalf of union general Scott conducted with Lee around the same time as the letter. The two quotes are often erroneously mashed up together.

49. Harriet Beecher Stowe, "Abraham Lincoln," written for the January 7, 1864, issue of *The Christian Watchman and Reflector*, quoted here from a reprint in *Littel's Living Age*, February 1864.

50. Francis B. Carpenter, *Six Months at the White House* (New York: Hurd and Houghton, 1866).

51. Reprinted here from "Recollections of President Lincoln." *Springfield Republican* (Springfield, MA), April 18, 1865.

52. Charles Chiniquy, *Fifty Years in the Church of Rome* (New York: Fleming H. Revel Co, 1886).

53. Two letters in the Lincoln Papers, Library of Congress.

54. Charles Hull, *Reflections from a Busy Life,* 1881.

55. Nathaniel Tallmadge, Appendix to *Spiritualism,* Vol 1. (New York: Partridge and Brittan, 1853).

56. Adam Goodheart, *1861: The Civil War Awakening* (New York: Random House, 2011).

57. "Govennor's Message No. 1," *Charleston Daily Courier*, November 27, 1867.

58. *Declaration of the Secession of South Carolina from the Federal Union and the Ordinance of Secession, Printed By Order of the Convention.* (Charleston, SC: Evans and Cogwell, 1860).

59. Diary of Elisha Hunt Rhodes, September 30, 1862. Reprinted in *All For the Union: The Civil War Diary and Letters of Elisha Hunt Rhodes*, Vintage Civil War Library, 1992.

60. The Seventy-Second New York, incidentally, served under Daniel Sickles, who later confirmed that séances took place at the White House. Like most of the messages I checked into, though, the story didn't quite check out; the name John Hanley doesn't appear in 72nd New York registers. Often I would find a soldier (or soldiers) with the same name, but the other details wouldn't match.

61. "Message Department," *Banner of Light*, April 29, 1865.

62. Bishop Simpson's oration at Lincoln's funeral.

63. Robert Toth, "The Old Haunted House at 1600 Pennsylvania Ave," *Milwaukee Journal*, March 9, 1973.

64. John Day and Theodore Parker, (Spirit), *Biography of Mrs. J. H. Conant, The World's Medium of the 19th Century* (Boston: William White and Co., 2005).

65. Noah Brooks, *Washington in Lincoln's Time*. (New York: The Century Co., 1895).

66. *Newark Ohio Daily Advocate*, December 5, 1883.

67. Lincoln Papers, LOC.

68. "Mr. Lincoln and Big Eagle—A Crumb for the Spiritualists," *San Francisco Bulletin*, March 6, 1874.

69. ibid.

70. Lincoln Papers, LOC.

71. Jerome Big Eagle, "A Sioux Story of the War," 1894.

72. "Lincoln and the Spirits," *Saturday Evening Gazette,* Boston, April 25, 1863.

73. It's often said that the reporter's full name was Prior Melton. This presumably comes from confusing him with Melton Prior, a London war correspondent and journalist who would have only been 17 years old at in April of 1863.

74. "Melange," *Boston Saturday Evening Gazette*, June 6, 1863.

75. "Explanation," *Banner of Light*, Boston, June 20, 1863.

76. Taylor's spirit was followed by a spirit who identified himself as Theodore Chase, a Union veteran who died at Gettysburg and opened with a cheerful "Hiya! If I were to judge I would say that Jeff expected advice from a different source … here I am to-day, bringing up the rear of old Zach! I should be very

glad to have a good old-fashioned chat with my friends, provided they are not afraid of ghosts." The "messages" don't often hold up to research, but they're fascinating to read.

77. "Message Department," *Banner of Light*, May 13, 1865.

78. Illustration taken from Fayette Hall, *The Secret and Political History of the Rebellion* (New Haven: Fayette Hall, author and publisher, 1890).

79. Orville Hickman Browning, *The Diary of Orville Hickman Browning Volume 1, 1850–1864*, published by the Illinois State Historical Library, Springfield, IL, 1925. The entry occurred on the first page of the 1863 diary, which the editors of the volume describe as small volume bound in plum-colored leather.

80. "The Deed," *Chicago Times*, January 3, 1863.

81. Orville Hickman Browning, *The Diary of Orville Hickman Browning Volume 1, 1850-1864*. Published by the Illinois State Historical Library, Springfield, IL, 1925. The entry occurred on the first page of the 1863 diary, which the editors of the volume describe as small volume bound in plum-colored leather.

82. William H. Chaney, "Was President Lincoln a Spiritualist?" *Common Sense: A Journal of Live Ideas*, May 16, 1874.

83. William H. Chaney, "Was He a Spiritualist? Reminisces of President Lincoln," *Religion-Philosophical Journal*, January 16, 1886.

84. M. A. Laurie to Abraham Lincoln, December 19, 1864, Abraham Lincoln Papers, LOC.

85. Reprinted in "The Religious Convictions of Abraham Lincoln," *Religion-Philosophical Journal*, November 1885.

86. Brower, D. H. B. *Montour County, Pennsylvania: A Collection of Historical and Biographical Sketches* (Harrisburg, PA: Lane S. Hart, 1881).

87. "Law Suits Proceeds For Spiritualism," *Philadelphia Inquirer*, January 5, 1901.

88. Interestingly, he also appears in a fantastic ghost story from 1880—according to a *Grand Forks Herald* article from May 13 of that year, there was a stream known as Black Creek rolling through Luzerne County, Pennsylvania. According to the article, fish didn't live in it, and any frog tossed in would immediately die and float to the surface. "The mountain gap traversed by the stream is one of the most dismal places to be found ... it is almost always filled with a haze which sunbeams scarcely ever penetrate ... enormous snakes crawl over the rocks and bathe in slimy pools." A century before, it said, Black Creek had been beautiful. When a man who owned a cabin nearby mortally wounded a man, the man's sister, a black-eyed "witch" with long, raven hair, cursed the killer, turning the waters of the creek black. Thereafter, only one road passed by the place, and horses would stop dead as they passed it. Kase eventually built a railroad through the gap, and suffered no ill effects (unless you count all the lawsuits), but

a man who built a hotel on the grounds fell to ruin, and some blamed the curse of the witch.

89. Though Mr. Conklin's first initials changed between Kase's tellings, it is presumably the same Conklin whose seven-page letter of spiritual advice from Edward Baker are preserved in the Library of Congress's Lincoln Papers. By the time of Kase's story, tales that Lincoln had attended Conklin's seances in Washington had been going around in spiritualist circles for several years. He's also sometimes said to have predicted the assassination. Most of the stories began in 1872, a year after Conklin died. In his life, Conklin was the first to connect Lincoln to Spiritualism, telling the *Cleveland Plain Dealer* in 1860 that he recognized Lincoln from having attended his seances in New York.

90. "Col S. P. Kase as a Spiritualist," *The Columbian* (Bloomsburg, PA), August 15, 1879.

91. ibid.

92. Judge Wattles is a mystery himself—there were a few judges by that name over the years, but I can't definitively say that any of them were the man Kase spoke of.

93. S. P. Kase, in *Mind and Matter*, Philadelphia, April 5, 1879.

94. Mrs. M. E. Williams, "Abraham Lincoln, a Spiritualist," 1891 lecture.

95. I couldn't find the original *Sun* article, but it was also printed in the article "From the Other Shore" in the *Chicago Tribune*, June 3, 1888. A couple of weeks later it ran as "A Spook Story" in *The Indianapolis Sun. The New York Sun* article was probably from around that time.

96. S. P. Kase to Sam Watson, July 14, 1877. Reprinted in *American Spiritual Magazine,* Vol 3.

97. Congressional Serial Set Vol 1150, Memorial of S. P. Case on Behalf of Reading and Columbia Railroad Company, praying the construction of a railroad from Washington city to New York.

98. "Was Abraham Lincoln a Spiritualist?" *New Orleans Times-Picayune*, July 26, 1891.

99. *Mind and Matter*, May 17, 1879.

100. Quotes in this section, unless otherwise noted, are from Nettie Colburn Maynard, *Was Abraham Lincoln a Spiritualist?* Rufus T. Hartranft Publisher, Philadelphia. 1891.

101. "Mrs. Maynard Disavows," *Banner of Light,* Boston, May 16, 1891.

102. *The Carrier Dove*, May 1891.

103. *Banner of Light*, May 28, 1891.

104. Lincoln Papers, LOC.

105. "Spiritualism," *Daily Evening Telegraph* (Philadelphia, PA), August 23, 1866.

106. ibid.

107. John C. Bundy papers, University of Illinois at Chicago.

108. "Abraham Lincoln Not a Spiritualist," *Chicago Tribune*, October 22, 1891.

109. ibid.

110. B. O. Flower, "Books of the Day," *The Arena, Vol. 5*, Arena Publishing Co, 1892.

111. "Was Not a Medium," *Miner's Journal*, (Pottsville, PA), October 21, 1891.

112. Hudson Tuttle, "Was Lincoln a Spiritualist? Mrs. Colburn Maynard and her Critics," *Banner of Light*, November 21, 1891.

113. "Ghostly Musicians: George Garrett Sickles, On His Deathbed, Believes That He Sees and Hears Them," *Macon Telegraph* (Macon, GA), March 19, 1887, reprinting a *New York Sun* piece.

114. *Times*, Troy, NY, December 29, 1881.

115. "Lincoln's Prophetic Dream," *Cleveland Plain Dealer*, October 10, 1887 (reprinting a *Philadelphia Times* piece).

116. ibid.

117. "President Lincoln's Death," *Illinois State Register* (Springfield) November 10, 1883, reprinted a recent column from *The Liberal* (Nashville, TN).

118. "Deaths of Well-Known Printers," *New Orleans Times-Picayune*, February 21, 1886.

119. W. S. Bailey's 1886 obituary in *Progress: A Monthly Magazine of Advanced Thought* vol 6.

120. In a particularly amusing anecdote from the attack, she wrote in *The Index* in 1886 that that her sister Ella poured a barrel of yellow paint on an attacker from a second floor window. He rushed upstairs, demanding to see the man who threw paint on him, Ella said "I am the man." He said, "It is a good thing for you that you're not a mam." She replied "And it is a *good thing* for you that I am *not* a man." There's also an 1857 item in a paper saying that Bailey, the "abolitionist" editor, had been egged out of Alexandria, Virginia. He also attended the 1856 Republican Convention, along with Owen Lovejoy, the source of one of Lincoln's fatal premonitions.

121. Ward Hill Lamon, edited by Dorothy Lamon Teillard. *Recollections of Abraham Lincoln.* "Published by the Editor" Washington, DC, 1911.

122. "Mourning: further details of the terrible tragedy at Washington—interesting incidents of Mr. Lincoln's last days," *New York Herald*, April 18, 1865.

123. Gideon Welles, *Diary: Vol 2.* Published by Houghton Mifflin, 1911.

124. Gideon Welles, article in *The Galaxy*, April, 1872.

125. Joseph Barrett, *Abraham Lincoln and his Presidency.* (Cincinnati, OH: Robert Clarke Co, 1904).

126. Frederick Seward, *Seward at Washington* (New York: Derby and Miller, 1891).

127. Ward Hill Lamon, edited by Dorothy Lamon Teillard. *Recollections of Abraham Lincoln.* "Published by the Editor" Washington, DC, 1911.

128. "Our Dead President in Philadelphia," *Philadelphia Inquirer*, April 24, 1865.

129. Abraham Lincoln to Mary Lincoln. June 9, 1863.

130. Crook, Col. William. "Through Five Administrations," Harper and Bros, New York, 1909

131. Elizabeth Keckley, *Behind the Scenes, or, Thirty Years a Slave, and Four Years in the White House* (New York: G. W. Carlton and Co, 1868).

132. ibid.

133. "He Scented Danger," *Biloxi Daily Herald*, January 8, 1904.

134. This story has been repeated in several books, but I couldn't find a good source that confirmed all the details at once. Thomas Eckert, at one time secretary of war, worked in the assassination investigations, and did say in a House of Representatives questioning in 1867 that Lewis Payne, a co-conspirator, had made a statement that Booth had been with him at the speech and tried to get him to shoot him right then, but he refused, and that an enraged Booth had wandered around after the speech saying "That's the last speech he will ever make."

Other early accounts have Booth turning to David Herold, a different co-conspirator, and saying "That means nigger citizenship. Now, by God! I'll put him through." This version comes from Frederick Stone, Herold's counsel. The common story conflates the two accounts. Herold and Payne were both with Booth at the time, so it's possible that he said one thing to one man and one to the other.

135. Joan Zyda, "The Haunting Reminders at Ford's Theatre," *Chicago Tribune*, October 5, 1976.

136. ibid.

137. Leslie Carpenter, "Washington Beat," *Boston Herald*, January 21, 1968.

138. "Ford's Theatre Spooks," *The Palm Beach Post*, May 6, 1976.

139. "Taint of the Goblin: it still clings to some historic houses in Washington," *Idaho Statesman* (Boise), January 31, 1894.

140. "Ford's Theatre Spooks," *The Palm Beach Post*, May 6, 1976.

141. Booth's diary, incidentally, is quite a read. Pondering his fate, he says "I have too great a soul to die like a criminal." Goodness, what an asshole.

142. "Assassination of President Lincoln and Sec Seward! The President shot in the theatre, Mr. Seward stabbed," *Albany Evening Journal*, April 15, 1865.

143. Samuel J. Seymour, (as told to Frances Spatz Leighton). "I Saw Lincoln Shot," *The Milwaukee Sentinel*, February 7, 1954.

144. Timothy Good, *We Saw Lincoln Shot: One Hundred Eyewitness Accounts* (Jackson, MS: University Press of Mississippi, 1995).

145. Finis Bates, *The Escape and Suicide of John Wilkes Booth* (Memphis, TN: The Historical Publishing Co., 1907).

146. Classified ad, *Denver Post*, March 3, 1901.

147. "Arrives! Prof. Bentley Sage," *Fort Worth Star-Telegram*, April 5, 1905.

148. Page 11, John Wilkes Booth FBI file, letter dated January 10, 1925.

149. "The Lost Slayer of John Wilkes Booth Who Came to Kansas," *Kansas City Star*, June 1, 1913.

150. Quotes in this section, unless noted, come from "Ghostly Communings," *Chicago Tribune*, March 5, 1866.

151. Timothy Good, *We Saw Lincoln Shot: One Hundred Eyewitness Accounts* (Jackson, MS: University Press of Mississippi, 1995).

152. no headline, *Cleveland Leader*, September 23, 1870.

153. "Lincoln's Shade Appears," *Pawtucket Times*, March 27, 1905.

154. Dave Ginsburg, "Grandpa's Ghost Stirs Mudd House," Associated Press (here from *New Haven Morning Star*, October 23, 1983).

155. "Hung!" *Philadelphia Inquirer*, July 8, 1865.

156. "Christian Rath, Now 84, Tells How He Personally Executed Four of President Lincoln's Assassinators," *Jackson Citizen Patriot*, February 12, 1914.

157. Karen Peterson, "When Ghosts Walk, Watch the White House," *The Oregonian*, October 29, 1971.

158. John Alexander, *Washington Ghosts* (Washington: Washington Books, 1975).

159. ibid.

160. "Martyred Mrs. Surratt," *Cleveland Plain Dealer*, June 25, 1878.

161. "Mrs. Surratt's House Haunted," *Macon Weekly Telegaph*, December 24, 1866.

162. Claudia De Lys, *8414 Strange and Fascinating Superstitions* (Castle Books, 1948).

163. "One Puzzle Solved," *Harrisburg Patriot*, November 22, 1888.

164. ibid.

165. ibid.

166. "Nothing to Do with Lincoln," *Indianapolis Journal*, November 24, 1901.

167. *Seeger and Guernsey's Cyclopaedia of the Manufactures and Products of the United States* (New York: The Seeger and Guernsey Co., 1890).

168. Isaac Newton Arnold, *Life of Abraham Lincoln* (Chicago: McClurg and Co., 1884). Mary Lincoln told this story to Isaac Newton Arnold in an 1874 interview.

169. Which exact cemetery they were in does not seem to be known, though Richmond's Hollywood Cemetery is on the banks of the James River. Lincoln was not buried there, of course, but Jefferson Davis eventually was—it's fascinating to imagine that perhaps Abraham and Mary had this talk on the grounds where Davis would one day lie. But even in 1865, Hollywood Cemetery was hardly a country graveyard.

170. The original design of the Capitol called for a glass floor in which visitors could see Washington's tomb two floors down. The crypt was built, but not used, as Washington remains interred at Mt. Vernon. Until recently the crypt served a sort of grisly storage room for the catafalque on which Lincoln's coffin was held; the catafalque is still used for all coffins laid in state in the rotunda, and was long kept in the crypt when not in use (Well, where else are you gonna keep it?). It's currently visible in the exhibit hall of the Capitol visitor's center.

171. Legislative *New Orleans Times-Picayune,* April 26, 1865.

172. Lloyd Lewis, *Myths After Lincoln* (Champaign-Urbana: Carl Sandburg Collections Library, University of Illinois, 1941).

173. "The City: The President's Funeral," *Chicago Tribune,* May 2, 1865.

174. John Hay and John Nicolay, "Abraham Lincoln: A History," *The Century Illustrated Monthly Magazine, Vol. 39*, November 1889.

175. William E. Axon, *The Ancoats Skylark and Other Verses.* John Heywood, Manchester, UK 1894.

176. *Frank Leslie's Illutrated Newspaper*, January 4, 1868.

177. "The Court House Ghost: An Important Revolution— He Is Described," *Chicago Tribune*, December 20, 1867.

178. "Waiting for the Train," The *Albany Daily Evening Times*, March 23, 1872.

179. Harold Whitman, "Keeper of the Great," *Cleveland Plain Dealer*, February 10, 1946.

180. There is an urban legend that Lincoln's voice was recorded by Edouard-Leon Scott de Martinville, who had devised way to record sounds onto paper, though not a way to play them back, but that Lincoln's recording had been lost. de Martinville was a real person, and modern technology has now allowed some of his recordings to be played, but there's no evidence that he actually recorded Lincoln.

181. "Lincoln Shrine Remodeling is Difficult Task," *Daily Illinois State Journal*, July 6, 1930.

182. "And His Face was Chalky White," *LIFE*, February 16, 1963.

183. "Recalls Look at Lincoln's Face in Tomb," *Chicago Tribune*, February 6, 1962.

184. Lloyd Lewis, *Myths After Lincoln* (Champaign-Urbana: Carl Sandburg Collections Library, University of Illinois, 1941).

185. Philip Kinsley, "Old Legends Surround New Tomb," *Chicago Tribune,* June 28, 1931.

186. "To Move Body of R. T. Lincoln's Son," *Daily Illinois State Journal,* May 25, 1930.

187. "Lincoln Crypts," *Daily Illinois State Journal,* November 8, 1931.

188. Harry Houdini, "How I Unmask the Spirit Fakers," *Popular Science,* November 1925.

189. The date was pinpointed from a footnote specifying that Schurz's meeting at the White House was on June 8 in *The Papers of Andrew Johnson Vol. 8,* (University of Tennessee Press, 1989).

190. Carl Schurz, *The Reminisces of Carl Schurz, Volume 3* (London: John Murray, 1909).

191. ibid.

192. ibid.

193. "Messages Department," *Banner of Light,* March 16, 1867.

194. No headline. *Providence Evening Press,* August 16, 1875.

195. "Katie King," *Chicago Daily Inter Ocean,* August 1, 1874.

196. "Spiritual Clap Trap," *Quincy Whig,* October 8, 1874.

197. "Dead Men in Politics: Ghosts to Form New Party That is to Sweep the Country," *New York Herald*, July 16, 1888.

198. "Chicagoans Remarkable Discovery in Literature," *Chicago Tribune,* January 14, 1888.

199. "Treading on Belva's Toes," *Boston Herald*, August 2, 1888.

200. "Spiritualist Sees Lincoln Working on Roosevelt!" *Daily People* (New York), September 19, 1910.

201. "Frauds in Spirit Pictures," *New York Herald*, November 11, 1895.

202. William Mumler, *Personal Experiences of William H. Mumler in Spirit Photography* (Boston: Colby and Rich, 1875).

203. C. M. P. "Spirit Photographs: A New and Interesting Development," *Herald of Progress*, October 1862.

204. ibid.

205. Phineas T. Barnum, *Humbugs of World* (New York: Carleton, 1866).

206. "Spirit Photographs," *New York Herald*, April 13, 1869.

207. Quotes from the trial are from "Carnival at the Tombs," *New York Commercial Advertiser*, April 28, 1869, unless otherwise noted.

208. Oddly, a column of mixed news from New York in the April 17, 1869 *Springfield Republican* mentions Mumler's trial, followed by an item about J. B. Conklin letting Edgar Allan write through him, and then an item supposed

piano rider Daniel Sickles's opinions on General Grant, an odd case of three people from this book showing up in the same short column of random news items for no particular reason.

209. "Ghosts at the Tombs," *New York Commercial Advertiser*, May 3, 1869.

210. Quoted here from a reprint in *Savannah Daily Advertiser*, March 1, 1872.

211. "Mrs. Abraham Lincoln Sits for a Spirit Picture," *Boston Herald*, February 27, 1872.

212. William Mumler, *Personal Experiences of William H. Mumler in Spirit Photography* (Boston: Colby and Rich, 1875).

213. Dean Jauchius and James Rhodes, *The Trial of Mary Todd Lincoln* (New York: The Bobbs-Merill Co, 1959).

214. "Mrs. Lincoln's Derangement," *New York Evangelist*, May 27, 1875.

215. "Clouded Reason. Trial of Mrs. Abraham Lincoln for Insanity," *Chicago Tribune*, May 20, 1875.

216. ibid.

217. ibid.

218. "Mrs. Lincoln: An Attempt at Suicide," *Chicago Tribune*, May 21, 1875.

219. M. E. Williams, *Abraham Lincoln a Spiritualist*, pamphlet circa 1890, taken from an earlier *Mercury* newspaper that couldn't identified.

220. Susan M. Haake, Personal Interview, September 17, 2014.

221. "The Ghost of Lincoln Visits Mount Pleasant," *Daily Iowa State Register*, July 1, 1869.

222. Jane Polonsky, "History and Mystery Blend for Fort Monroe Tour," *Richmond Times-Dispatch*, April 2, 1972.

223. Quoted here via "Lincoln Haunted Loudonville," *Schenectady Gazette*, October 31, 1989.

224. "Colonel Rathbone's Mania," *New York Tribune*, December 31, 1883.

225. Letter from Clara Harris, reprinted first in "Lincoln's Last Days," *New York Independent*, April 29 1865, reprinted here from "We Saw Lincoln Shot," ibid.

226. David Moye, "Seattle Attorney Andrew Basiago Claims U. S. Sent Him on Time Travels," *Huffington Post*, April 28, 2012. http://www.huffingtonpost.com/2012/04/28/andrew-basiago-seattle-attorney-time-travels_n_1438216.html?ncid=edlinkusaolp00000003.

227. "Doctor of Dying Lincoln is Still Living," *Boston Herald*, August 3, 1930.

228. Gilson Willets, *Inside History of the White House*, 1908.

229. Theodore Roosevelt to Henry Pritchett, December 14, 1904.

230. Ishbell Ross, *Grace Coolidge and her Era* (New York: Dodd, Mead and Co, 1962).

231. The line is quoted in *Washington Ghosts* by John Alexander; I could not locate the original article he was quoting.

232. Leslie Lieber, "The Legend of Ghosts in the White House." *Richmond Times-Dispatch*, April 25, 1954.

233. ibid.

234. Lillian Rogers Parks, *My Thirty Years Backstairs at the White House* (Fleet Publishing Co, 1961).

235. ibid.

236. ibid.

237. J. B. West, *Upstairs at the White House* (New York: Coward, McGann & Geoghegan, 1973).

238. ibid.

239. ibid.

240. "Trumans Near Return to White House," *Toledo Blade*, February 7, 1952.

241. Some of the quotes here come from 1998 articles quoting the story (though they were under the impression that Truman was talking to Murrow). It attracted only a little bit of press attention in 1955; a recording exists at the Truman Presidential Library.

242. "White House Creaks Recalled by Truman," *Aberdeen Daily News*, May 28, 1955.

243. Margaret Truman, "Margaret Truman's Own Story,"
      Greensboro Record, September 29, 1956.

244. Leslie Lieber "The Legend of Ghosts in the White
      House," *Richmond Times-Dispatch*, April 25, 1954.

245. John Alexander, *Washington Ghosts* (Washington:
      Washington Book, 1975).

246. "Blind Children Enjoy Tour with Guide Julie," *The
      Spokesman-Review* (Spokane), November 9, 1971.

247. "Susan Ford Reports on White House," *Schenectady
      Gazette*, August 28, 1975.

248. "Billiards Racking Up Fans in Family Rooms of America."
      Pottstown Mercury (Pottstown, PA), February 27, 1975.

249. "White House Has Its Share of Stories," *Augusta
      Chronicle*, November 1, 2003.

250. "First Dog Sniffs Out Lincoln," *Boston Herald*, February
      12, 1986.

251. "Reagan Hopes for Special Meeting," *Boston Herald*,
      October 6, 1986.

252. Nancy Reagan, *My Turn* (New York: Random House,
      1989).

253. "Do Ghosts Haunt the White House?" *The Nation*,
      November 1997.

254. "First Lady: White House is Awe-Inspiring Place,"
      Rockford Register-Star, February 4, 1997.

255. "Cultivation of Fraternity," *Chicago Times*, April 12,
      1865.